William Shakespeare's
THE TEMPEST

Ralph A. Ranald
Assistant Dean, College of Arts and Science
New York University

This edition published by Barnes & Noble, Inc.,
by arrangement with Macmillan Publishing USA,
a division of Simon & Schuster, Inc.

1998 Barnes & Noble Books

MACMILLAN is a registered trademark of Macmillan, Inc.
Monarch and colophons are trademarks of Simon & Schuster, Inc.,
registered in the U.S. Patent and Trademark Office.

Macmillan Publishing USA
A division of Simon & Schuster, Inc.
1633 Broadway
New York, NY 10019

ISBN 0-7607-1016-3

Text design by Tony Meisel

Printed and bound in the United States of America.

98 99 00 01 02 03 M 9 8 7 6 5 4 3 2 1

RRDC

CONTENTS

INTRODUCTION TO WILLIAM SHAKESPEARE

The earliest documented fact about William Shakespeare is in the Parish Register of the Church of Stratford-on-Avon, which lists the date of Shakespeare's christening as April 26, 1564. Since it was customary to christen babies at the age of three days, scholars consider Shakespeare's birth date to be April 23, 1564. This date of birth is supported by the fact that Shakespeare is believed to have died on his birthday anniversary, and the date of his death appears on his monument as April 23, 1616. The dramatist was the third child of a family well known in the area. His father, John Shakespeare, was a merchant, and his mother came from a well-established land-owning family in Warwickshire, where Stratford is situated. The family prospered, and John Shakespeare rose to a high position in the administration of the town. Unfortunately, his financial situation declined; in 1587, he was removed from his position on the city council, and he seems to have had financial troubles until his death in 1601.

In the meantime, William Shakespeare was growing up in Stratford, then a town of about two thousand inhabitants—more important economically then than now. Traveling dramatic companies apparently stopped there, and it is possible that Shakespeare saw them. It was an important market town and boasted a good grammar school, which Shakespeare probably attended. Like most Elizabethan schoolboys, he must have learned Latin and probably some Greek. By the time he left school, he would have had to be fairly proficient in Latin. He did not go to university, possibly because of the financial reverses of his father.

The next important document concerning Shakespeare is a special marriage license issued on November 27, 1582, for the marriage of William Shakespeare and Anne Hathaway, a woman eight years his senior. The couple's first child was born in May 1583. Twins, named Hamnet and Judith, were born in 1585.

From 1585 to 1592, no documents about Shakespeare exist. This period in his life is referred to as "the lost years." Certainly Shakespeare had been in Stratford in 1584, and probably again in 1585, for the christening of the twins. John Aubrey, the seventeenth-century antiquarian and gossip, said that "Shakespeare had been, in his younger years, a schoolmaster in the country." Aubrey is not a trustworthy source. Another theory has Shakespeare participating in the wars against the Spanish in the Low Countries, while yet another has him in London, where his initial job was that of holding horses for theatergoers. Probably the most frequently heard story about Shakespeare during this time concerns his hurried departure from Stratford after he allegedly had stolen some deer from the park of Sir Thomas Lucy of Charlecote. All these stories should be treated with caution. In 1592 Shakespeare reappears in documents, most notably in a pamphlet written by the university wit, playwright, and journalist Robert Greene on his deathbed. Greene attacked Shakespeare for his presumption in competing with his betters in playwrighting. Undoubtedly, Shakespeare was by this time a threat to the university types also trying to make their living with their pens.

For the rest of his working life, Shakespeare wrote for and acted with a single dramatic company, The Lord Chamberlain's Company, known as the "King's Men" after the accession of James I. All of Shakespeare's thirty-seven plays were written for this group, who performed them in public theaters, and private theaters, private houses, and at court. Shakespeare provided them with one or two plays a year until 1612–1613, and he also shared in the profits.

How much of his time Shakespeare spent in London and how much in Stratford is not known. He was probably in Stratford for the funeral of his son Hamnet in 1596 and possibly for that of his father in 1601. His financial affairs seem to have been well managed. He invested heavily in Stratford real estate; in 1597, he bought New Place, one of the finest houses in town. He probably returned to Stratford permanently about 1610, but his work was not finished, as two more complete plays and parts of two others were written after that year.

The actual circumstances of Shakespeare's death are not known; his monument gives the date as April 23, 1616. A common belief is that Shakespeare died of a fever contracted at a merry meeting with the dramatist Ben Jonson and the poet Michael Drayton. Shakespeare's will left bequests to his two daughters, his friends and partners in the King's Men, and his wife. The oft-discussed bequest to Anne of the "second-best bed" has been taken to mean that the writer's marriage was unhappy, but such bequests were common, and, further, that bed was probably the one in which they slept.

THE ANTI-STRATFORDIANS

Possibly because of the fragmentary evidence concerning the life of Shakespeare, an anti-Shakespeare, or anti-Stratfordian, school of thought has developed. Followers of this school believe that Shakespeare was too uneducated to have written the plays himself, and a subtle snobbery seems to dictate that any candidate put forward as the real Shakespeare must be of birth and education superior to his. Suggested authors of Shakespeare's plays include Christopher Marlowe, Francis Bacon, the Earl of Southampton, the Earl of Oxford, and Sir Walter Raleigh. The Baconian and the Oxford theories are the two most popular, but most scholars prefer to accept Shakespeare as the creator of the plays that bear his name.

THE TEXT OF SHAKESPEARE'S PLAYS

Some of Shakespeare's plays were published during his lifetime. The texts published were of two kinds: (1) plays sold to printers by the King's Men, usually when the company needed money because the theaters were closed because of the plague; (2) pirated plays, or stolen and unauthorized texts, which were often inaccurate, and sometimes issued by unscrupulous printers who wanted to cash in on the popularity of a play. Both kinds were usually printed in modest-sized volumes and called "quartos," a word designating the size of the pages. The first kind of authorized text is usually called a "good quarto" and the pirated text a "bad quarto." Sometimes, a bad quarto was followed by the publication of a good quarto. Shakespeare's complete works were published in a large folio volume in 1623 by two of Shakespeare's friends, John Heminges and Henry Condell. Most of the comedies discussed here appeared in print for the first time in 1623.

THE PUBLIC THEATER OF SHAKESPEARE'S DAY

Shakespeare's theater was quite different from our own. It was an octagonal, or round, structure with three tiers of roofed galleries around the major section. The central portion was an unroofed yard, the "pit," in which spectators stood. These "standing room only" places cost the least (one penny—later, twopence), and the people who stood were often scornfully referred to as "groundlings"; they were believed by the more educated people to like nothing but clowning. This belief is not entirely supported by evidence. The roofed galleries, which contained seats, cost more the higher up the seat; by 1596, young gallants were sitting on the stage itself. Both men and women went to the theater, but boys played all the women's roles in the plays. The stage projected almost thirty feet into the yard and was narrower at the front than at the back. The back half of the stage was roofed with thatch; the other half left open. There was no proscenium arch and no front curtain, but there were curtains at the back between two sets of swinging doors placed at an angle to the stage. The curtain at the stage level formed the "inner stage" or "study," in which furniture properties were sometimes used, such as the bed in *Othello.* Above the study, a projecting balcony was built with a curtain about four feet behind it, forming another inner stage. The balcony, or "tarras," was useful for action such as the balcony scene in *Romeo and Juliet.* Open windows were set on the upper level over the doors, and they, too, could be used. Above the tarras, there was a smaller balcony with a railing and a curtain, used as a musicians' gallery or for the upper deck of a ship. A collection of three gabled structures, the "huts," was on the very top of this structure, creating a fourth level from which sound effects could be produced and from which objects such as thrones could be lowered onto the stage. Above the huts a flagstaff held the flag of the theater, which was flown during performances. Behind the stage was the "tiring house," or dressing room for the actors, while underneath the stage was the "hell," which had machinery for raising and lowering the stage trapdoors. In all, there were seven separate playing levels on the flexible Elizabethan stage.

Performances, announced with trumpet calls in the afternoon, started about two o'clock and lasted approximately two hours. Daylight was the only illumination in the public theaters, though candlelight was used for indoor performances at court and in the private theaters. The capacity of the theater varied with the individual building; it is probable that the Globe, Shakespeare's theater, held between two and three thousand people. The building was rarely filled to capacity except for a new play.

There were many advantages to this kind of theater, and the physical characteristics of the building and the stage helped to dictate the form of the plays. Since there was no scenery, the stage represented any place the playwright chose. As a result, the action moved quickly from place to place and from scene to scene so that alternation of plot and subplot was much simpler than it is today. Also, the action could take place on several different playing levels. Elizabethan plays were, therefore, swift moving and enhanced with poetry and everchanging action rather than hampered by scenery. Since there was no attempt at literal staging, sight and sound effects were evocative rather than realistic. Further, the playwright, with language alone, was able to establish the scenery in the imagination of the audience, though he could not employ physical sets.

SHAKESPEARE'S WORK

Shakespeare's work falls into four periods. The first, 1590–1594, includes history plays and the early farces, *The Comedy of Errors* and *The Taming of the Shrew*, as well as the early romantic comedies, The *Two Gentlemen of Verona* and *Love's Labour Lost.* The second, 1595–1600, includes additional history plays, the great comedies, and *The Merry Wives of Windsor.* The third, 1600–1608, is the period of Shakespeare's great tragedies and three "problem plays," of which *All's Well That Ends Well* is an example. Even in comedy, Shakespeare seems to be concerned with the darker aspects of the human spirit, and it is only because *All's Well* and its companion piece, *Measure for Measure*, end happily that they are classified as comedies. The works of the final period, 1609–1613, seem totally different in tone from the former works. This is the time when Shakespeare is writing dramatic romances such as *The Winter's Tale.* The playwright is creating a new, symbolic kind of drama extremely subtle in its presentation of ideas. These late romances always contain elements of tragedy but conclude in reconciliation.

INTRODUCTION TO *THE TEMPEST*

GENERAL

The Tempest, although one of Shakespeare's shortest and most compressed plays, is perhaps the most difficult to interpret. The play defies analysis and has given rise to odd interpretations. Often it has been seen as a religious or historical allegory, sometimes on the flimsiest of evidence. It is equally as often identified with Shakespeare's own life and especially with his farewell to his art and to the English stage.

Before we begin scene-by-scene study of *The Tempest,* let us look at aspects of this play that are particularly interesting or puzzling.

THE UNITIES

Structurally, the most important thing about *The Tempest* is that for once Shakespeare adhered rigidly to the three unities of classical drama described by Aristotle, his followers, and especially Horace, the Roman satirist and literary theorist.

The three unities were those of time, place, and action. In most of his plays Shakespeare was lax in observing the unities, and it has sometimes been thought that in *The Tempest* he observed them to show his friend and critic Ben Jonson that he was capable of doing so if he wished.

According to the unity of time, all of the action in a play should be confined as closely as possible within the course of a single day. Purists insisted that a play last exactly as long as the action on the stage, with no time lapses at all. It appears that *The Tempest* covers no more than four hours, because there does not appear to be within it the interval of a single night. Throughout the play Shakespeare makes constant references to the passage of time so as to make the time element conspicuous.

The unity of place is easily perceived. Everything, except the storm in Act I, Scene 1, takes place on a supposedly deserted island, and this storm takes place so close to the island that it really qualifies under the concept of the unity of place. This unity of place is exceptionally well observed in the play.

Finally, there is the unity of action. This means that no irrelevancies should be permitted in the course of the play and consequently all subplots and digressions should be avoided. Shakespeare has something of a subplot in the persons of Stephano, Trinculo, and possibly Caliban, but at the same time these characters are all tied together by the plot against the master of the enchanted island, Prospero.

The original purpose of the three unities may have been to increase artistic truth—the ability of a work of art to convince us that it represents reality. Since *The Tempest*, among all of Shakespeare's plays, is the most fantastic and improbable, employing many elements of magic and the supernatural, the observance of the unities here helps the audience to suspend disbelief in the marvels.

THE MASQUE ELEMENT IN *THE TEMPEST*

There is an element of masque in the play—i.e., a great deal of singing, dancing, supernatural machinery, and romantic unreality. But a masque implied an antimasque—usually a dance of satyrs or other clumsy and fantastic personalities. This is where Caliban comes in; he and the other characters of the subplot represent an antimasque. A banquet was also common material in a masque, and its vanishing was another piece of stagecraft for the wonder of Shakespeare's audience. Within *The Tempest* a wedding-masque is performed in Act IV at the betrothal of Ferdinand and Miranda.

THE DATE OF THE PLAY

The Tempest is generally dated 1611. It was performed at the English court to celebrate the marriage of the daughter of James I (reigned 1603–1625), the Princess Elizabeth, to the Elector of the Palatine. The marriage is dated 14 February 1613 (new style). The play celebrates fertility, and thus it is interesting to note that while the Elector and his wife sat on their thrones for a brief period and then spent the rest of their lives in exile, they did a great deal for the royal houses of Europe, providing many heirs to thrones and dukedoms. The first performance of the play seems on good authority to have been at court in 1611.

SOURCES OF THE PLAY

There are a number of possible sources for the play, none absolutely established. One source involves the founding of America. A boat carrying Sir George Somers, Admiral Sir Christopher Newport, who was one of the first founders of Virginia, and Sir Thomas Gates, the new Governor of the Virginia colony, was lost en route from Plymouth to Jamestown. It was cast away on the Bermudas (the "still-vexed Bermoothes" of *The Tempest*) on July 28, 1609. The shipwrecked men built a smaller boat and sailed to Virginia. The adventure was reported back in England, leading to the publication of Silvester Jourdan's account of the wreck called *A Discovery of the Barmudas*, otherwise called the Isle of Divels (1610). There is also another account, by William Strachey, dated July 15, 1610, though apparently not published until 1625; it is possible that Shakespeare saw it in manuscript form.

It is thought that the character Caliban comes from the essay of Michael de Montaigne called "Of the Cannibales." Hakluyt's *Voyages and Principall Navigations* is also a possible source, as is a play known as *The Fair Sidea* (*Die Schone Sidea*), written by the German playwright Jacob Ayrer some time before 1605. None of these may really be called the major source of *The Tempest.*

ALLEGORY AND THEME IN *THE TEMPEST*

One major theme of *The Tempest* is the growth of the human spirit. Shakespeare's contemporaries felt that each person's soul had three faculties or parts: sensible, rational, and intellectual. (This notion can be traced to the ancient Greek philosophers, especially Plato and Aristotle, as well as to ancient Judaeo-Christian tradition.) It may be suggested that Caliban, Stephano, and Trinculo represent the lowest, or sensible level of the soul (pertaining to sense or experience, lacking intellect). The various courtiers, along with Ferdinand and Miranda, may be equated with the higher or rational faculty. Finally Prospero, with his principal servant, Ariel, may be equated with pure intellect, or that highest quality of the soul found in a person at his or her best and in the angels. If this interpretation is accepted, we have an allegorical play showing the defeat and subduing of the two lower powers of the soul by the all-powerful one of intellect. Shakespeare does not carry this notion out completely. There are other, similar analyses of the meaning of *The Tempest.* It must be kept in mind that Shakespeare was also writing simply to entertain there is something in *The Tempest* for almost every possible audience.

Much of the interpretation of *The Tempest* centers around the characters of Prospero and his two strange servants Ariel and Caliban. Prospero is so much the director of all characters and all events on the enchanted island that he is continuously before the audience—even when he is not physically present on stage, he affects everything and everybody in the action.

DETAILED ANALYSIS

ACT I

ACT I: SCENE 1

The play opens with a storm at sea. In the midst of the storm is a ship furiously driven by the wind and rain; the entire first scene takes place on the deck of this ship, which is in danger of sinking at any moment.

The Master of the ship calls his Boatswain, who as the officer in charge of the sails and rigging must make every effort to save the ship. The fury of the storm is such that it might drive the ship onto a shore where it could be wrecked; therefore, the Boatswain calls upon the sailors of the crew to "fall to't yarely," i.e., work hard to take in the sails. It should be remembered that this storm, which we learn later is supernatural in origin, has come up very suddenly; the sailors have not been prepared for it.

As the sailors do all they can to make the ship secure against the storm, Alonso, King of Naples, appears on deck with his son, Ferdinand, who is heir to the throne; they are accompanied by Antonio, Duke of Milan; Sebastian, the brother of Alonso; and Gonzalo, an honest adviser and councilor to Alonso.

Alonso advises the Boatswain to "Play the men." The word "play" here has been interpreted as "ply," which would mean that Alonso is ordering the Boatswain to make the men work; it is implied that Alonso and the other passengers are not prepared to trust the skill of the officers and sailors of the ship.

The furious activity of the crew in attempting to save the ship at first does not impress Alonso and his friends. The Boatswain wishes only that they would go back to their cabins. "You mar our labors," he tells them. The Boatswain adds, to Gonzalo: "What cares these roarers for the name of King?" He means that the winds and waves of the storm will not listen to the King if he should tell them to be quiet, and therefore the King and his party should go below and leave the sailors to fight the storm. The conversation with the Boatswain makes this clear.

There is ill feeling between the crew and their passengers; thus, as the Boatswain shouts his orders and tells the King and his party to get out of the way, Antonio says to the Boatswain: "We are less afraid to be drowned than thou art." Antonio does not trust the crew's skill and shows it. Gonzalo seems to accept whatever happens philosophically; he is even mildly humorous in his reference to the Boatswain as having a complexion "of perfect gallows." Gonzalo says at several points that it is obvious to him that the Boatswain looks like a man fated to die by hanging. Since the Boatswain will be hanged upon a gallows on dry land, he cannot die by drowning. In the circumstances, this is Gonzalo's idea of a joke.

Suddenly the sailors come in wet, shouting that all is lost and that the only thing anyone can do now is to pray. Antonio is angry; he believes that the crew has not done enough. "We are merely (i.e., simply) cheated of our lives by drunkards," which means that Antonio believes that the crew has been drunk and not capable of doing its best. As Scene 1 ends, the sailors are shouting that the ship is about to sink. Gonzalo has the last word: "The wills above be done! But I would fain die a dry death." "The wills above" refers to the will of God or of the divine powers who, in the terms of the play, are responsible for a person's destiny. At the same time, Gonzalo can wish that things were different on board this ship, which is evidently sinking.

COMMENT

With the very first lines of the play, two pairs of opposites are suggested. These are:

1. Tempest, or Storm—as opposed to Calm.
2. The Power of a King—as opposed to Other Kinds of Natural or Supernatural Power.

The first pair is easy to understand, as it is represented on the stage physically. The second arises from the fact that Alonso, the King, attempts to give orders which he has no business giving. He is a King, but on a ship he is just a passenger, and he must entrust his life to those whose business it is to sail the ship.

The Boatswain tells the King and his companions that if they have "authority" over the winds and waves, then he too will obey them. Otherwise, while the King may be King on land, the order of nature on board the ship tends to make everyone equal in fighting for his life, and power to command can go only to those who have the skill. This point is important, and we will encounter it all through *The Tempest*, for much of the play is about power—its use and abuse.

The idea that what happens to humans is in some way controlled by a higher power is raised at the end of Scene 1 by Gonzalo, who in many ways is an interpreter of the play. At the same time, Gonzalo implies, humans have both a will of their own and the power and duty to help themselves. This idea is also developed in later scenes.

SUMMARY

By this short scene of only sixty-three lines, Shakespeare has brilliantly brought the reader or viewer into the midst of the action and raised suspense to a high pitch as we wonder what will happen to those on the ship. At the same time, various pairs of opposing concepts have been introduced.

1. Tempest, or Storm as opposed to Calm.
2. The Power of a King as opposed to other kinds of Natural or Supernatural Power.
3. Fate as opposed to a Human's Freedom to Act in Order to Save His or Her Life.
4. The Human as opposed to Nature

These opposites are only hinted at in this scene. There is one final idea even more shadowy than these: the tempest itself is more than a physical storm at sea. In some way, it comes to reflect a certain disarrangement and disorder in the human spirit; therefore, there is a fifth pair of opposites that we can find in Scene 1:

5. Order as opposed to Disorder.

The order is in man himself, in the assembly of men into a state governed by a King or ruler, and in Nature. These are the three important aspects of Shakespeare's universe as described in this play; the important point to remember is that as *The Tempest* opens, all three—Humans, the King, and Nature—are in a state of disorder.

ACT 1: SCENE 2

The second scene, which composes the rest of Act 1, is very long; it takes place entirely in Prospero's cell, the small room and library where he practices magic, on the enchanted island where most of the action of the play is set. The scene opens with an explanation of the origins of the storm. Miranda, daughter of Prospero, establishes her merciful character at the beginning as she asks her father, the creator of the tempest, to make the ship and all its people safe. She is afraid that all on the ship will be drowned. For Miranda has seen the ship. "O, I have suffered/ With those that I saw suffer . . ." She wishes those on the ship to be shown mercy.

Prospero reassures his daughter. Those on the ship will not be harmed; nobody on the ship will suffer "so much perdition as an hair," i.e., will not lose even a single hair from his head, so careful is Prospero of their safety as he works his magic on them.

Prospero then explains to Miranda who she is, and who he is. It becomes obvious that until this day she has not known their origins or how they got to the enchanted island. He removes his magic garment, apparently a costume that Prospero wears when he is practicing his magic. Reassuring Miranda: "Wipe thou thine eyes; have comfort," he explains the mystery of their origin.

The explanation proceeds through question and answer in such a way that the audience as well as Miranda becomes aware of the history of both of them. The audience is also told of the history of Antonio and Alonso.

Antonio is Prospero's brother, having taken the position of Duke of Milan away from Prospero and exiled both Prospero and Miranda to the island. Miranda makes it clear that in the past she has often wondered who she was and where she and her father had come from, but until this day her father had always put her off with excuses. Now Prospero will tell her.

He explains that twelve years previous to this day—he was the Duke of Milan—the position now occupied by his brother Antonio. He recalls the days "in the dark backward and abysm of time" when Miranda, as she vaguely remembers, had many servants and attendants, as did he. Miranda would have been so young that she wouldn't remember much of what had happened. Prospero reassures her that he is in fact her father and that he had been exiled to this lonely place with his daughter by the treachery of Antonio.

Prospero recalls that among all the "signories" (the states of Northern Italy), the Duke of Milan, himself, had been the greatest and most powerful. But because he studied the liberal arts and became a master of many arts and sciences, he thereby took less and less interest in governing his Dukedom. He turned over more and more of his power to his brother, Antonio. One day Antonio, this "false uncle" of Miranda, having secretly removed many of the men whom Prospero had appointed to positions of power, took over the government himself in all but name. He acted as ruler while Prospero still had the title of Duke.

Antonio's ambition grew; "he needs will be/ Absolute Milan," i.e., he wanted to be the Duke. He began to plan a way to get rid of his brother. (A King or Duke is sometimes called by the place which he rules, thus, Antonio is sometimes referred to simply as "Milan" rather than as "Duke of Milan.") The exercise of power corrupts Antonio; he wants to have all of his brother's power.

For Prospero, as he himself says, his library "was dukedom large enough." He withdrew from the world of action and of the governing of men into the world of ideas. Meanwhile his brother came to despise Prospero's abilities as a ruler and made an arrangement with Alonso, the King of Naples, "so dry was he for sway" (meaning: thirsty for power), whereby Antonio, in return for help in taking over the Dukedom of Milan, would pay homage to the King of Naples and acknowledge his power.

Miranda, in asking her father whether Antonio could really be his brother since he has done such a terrible thing, implies that any brother capable of acting in such a way is no real brother. Here we see the idea of nature as opposed to the unnatural, which is developed further in the play.

One night, after the agreement between Antonio and Naples has been concluded, Antonio opens the gates of Milan to an invading army. Antonio, the King of Naples, and their soldiers dared not harm Prospero and Miranda, because the people of Milan all loved Prospero:

> . . . they durst not So dear the love my people bore me; nor set A mark so bloody on the business . . .

Instead, they put the father and daughter to sea in "a rotten caress of a butt." (The "butt" is apparently a small boat, without masts or sails, in such poor repair that it is leaking.) Antonio assumes that his brother and his daughter will never be seen alive again. But Gonzalo, the noble courtier and adviser to Duke Prospero, saved their lives by placing both food and water, as well as clothing, books, and other necessaries, on the fragile boat in which Prospero and Miranda were set adrift. At this point, Prospero breaks off the story he is telling to Miranda. By his magic art, he puts Miranda to sleep; then he summons his attendant Spirit, Ariel.

Ariel appears at line 189 of this scene, returning to his master, Prospero, in the latter's cell. In this part of Scene 2, we learn through Ariel's report that he, Ariel, under the orders of Prospero, has caused the tempest. Further, it is made clear that while Prospero and Ariel deliberately frightened the sailors into believing that the ship was sinking, none of them was harmed. Ariel had leaped onto the ship and had "flamed amazement"; he had turned himself into flames, making eerie noises, and frightened the sailors so that some of them, believing that "all the devils are here," fell or jumped overboard. One of the first to leave the ship was the King's son, Ferdinand.

We learn further that all of the men are safe: "Not a hair perished." Indeed, not even their clothing is wet. The ship itself has by magic power been docked in a sort of cove or harbor, with most of the crew "charmed . . . under hatches stowed." The rest of the fleet, believing the King's ship lost, has gone sadly home toward Naples.

The first mention of the "still vexed Bermoothes" is made at this point (line 229). We shall return to this later, but it is thought that *The Tempest* was partly inspired by the account of a voyage to Bermuda. ("Still vexed" means "ever vexed, or troubled," "still" being an Elizabethan word for "always" or "ever.") Whatever places are referred to in the play, the actual place and its geography are not important. Shakespeare sets the action on an enchanted island, where the normal laws of Nature do not operate or, at any rate, seem to be modified by the enchantments and the magic arts of Prospero and those Spirits who assist him.

We realize, as Ariel makes his report, that the time is "at least two glasses," i.e., about two o'clock in the afternoon. Prospero, upon learning the time, says to Ariel that between the present and the time when his, Prospero's, work ends, he must finish what it is his intention to finish. As Prospero says (lines 240–241)

> The Time 'twixt six and now Must by us both be spent most preciously.

At line 242 and following, the dialogue informs us that Ariel desires freedom from Prospero. Ariel is a servant of Prospero, bound to serve him for a definite number of years. Prospero, Ariel reminds him, has promised to give Ariel his freedom early if the present work they are doing is successful:

> Thou did promise To bate me a full year.

Ariel means by this that Prospero promised to abate, or shorten, the term of his service by a year. Prospero reminds his servant that he, Prospero, rescued Ariel from the enchantments of "the foul witch Sycorax." This reminder, and the retelling by Prospero of the story of Sycorax and her son, Caliban, is part of the exposition of the play. In speaking of the torment from which he rescued Ariel, Prospero gives us much information that we must have if we are to understand the relationships among Prospero, Ariel, and Caliban. We also learn about Sycorax, who does not appear in the play. More important, we are given certain expectations as to what kind of a being Caliban is; he does not appear on the stage until he has been described and introduced by Prospero and Ariel as they discuss him.

Caliban's shape is not exactly human. Shakespeare leaves a good deal to our imagination, but apparently Caliban appears in part like a human being, in part like a fish, in part like a tortoise. Caliban is treated by Prospero not as a valued servant but as a slave; this is in contrast with Prospero's way of dealing with Ariel. Caliban is necessary in Prospero's service, but he is still a slave "whom stripes may move, not kindness." That is to say, he can be made obedient only by the threat of the whip.

One of the abilities of Ariel, which we accept by this time even though it is objectively fantastic, is his ability to travel anywhere almost instantaneously. Prospero makes this clear when he reproaches Ariel for his complaints:

> Dost thou forget From what a torment I did free thee? (lines 250–251).

Ariel answers, rhetorically, "no," whereupon Prospero continues to punish his servant verbally:

> Thou dost; and think'st it much to tread the ooze Of the salt deep, To run upon the sharp wind of the North, To do me business in the veins o'th' earth When it is baked with frost (lines 253–257).

The purpose of this interchange is twofold: it provides additional exposition for the drama, so that we will know what the action has been prior to the actual chronological beginning of *The Tempest* with the shipwreck, and it builds up the character of Ariel so that we suspend our disbelief in this fantastic creature.

It is best not to be too literal in one's analysis of Ariel. In the speech of Prospero quoted above, we find that Ariel has the ability of traveling within three of the four "elements" or fundamental substances that the Elizabethans believed to constitute the material universe: Earth, Water, Air, and Fire. Ariel can move in the "salt deep"; he runs upon the "sharp wind of the North"; he serves Prospero "in the veins o' th' earth." The elements referred to are obviously Water, Air, and Earth. As to Fire, Ariel changed himself into fire to terrify the sailors in Scene 1, and as we shall see, that is the element most akin to Ariel's own nature.

Prospero threatens Caliban with various punishments if he does not obey. At the same time, we learn much about Caliban's nature: he is resentful and believes that Prospero has taken away his rights:

> The island's mine by Sycorax my mother, Which thou tak'st from me (lines 331–332).

Here Prospero loses his patience with Caliban, pointing out to him that he treated him well until he betrayed this kindness by attempting to attack Miranda, an attack that Prospero prevented. Prospero had taught Caliban language and useful arts:

> I endowed thy purposes With words that made them known (lines 356–357).

But Caliban does not appreciate this and still struggles against his master.

In contrast to Ariel, Caliban is a creature of the earth. Remember that Prospero specifically addresses Caliban as "Slave! Caliban! Thou earth thou!" (Act I, Scene 2, lines 313–314). As one reads the entire second scene of Act I, the contrasting natures of Ariel and Caliban become more apparent. But both natures need to be guided, restrained, led or managed by Prospero. The threats that Prospero uses against Ariel are of a less menacing or physical nature than those he uses against Caliban, but in dealing with both he must use threats. Prospero is, however, a kindly man, a beneficent authority figure, and we are somehow not convinced that he would put into action the threats he utters against Ariel and Caliban.

Prospero once again reminds Ariel of "the damned witch Sycorax" from whom he, Prospero, rescued Ariel—her spell confined Ariel in a pine tree. The reference to "Argier" (Algiers), from which Sycorax had been banished for her witchcraft, is one more geographical reference that shows the fantastic nature of the enchanted island. Algiers and Bermuda are not close geographically, and yet the island where *The Tempest* is set seems to be in proximity to both—one more sign not to take the geography in it seriously.

Having recalled Ariel to his duty—not that Ariel seriously contemplated defying his master—Prospero goes to Caliban, while Ariel departs in the shape of a water nymph. The entire dialogue between Prospero and Caliban, lines 321–376, is interesting in a number of ways. First, it establishes further the character of Prospero and tends to confirm our view of him as the master of everything and everyone on the enchanted island. Second, it gives something of Caliban's history and establishes his character so that we can see why Prospero treats him as he does. Caliban is at once a humorous creature and one who has elements of pathos. He reproaches Prospero for having stolen his land: "This island's mine by Sycorax my mother. . . ." (line 331). The Elizabethan age was, of course, an age of discovery and exploration. English mariners such as Drake, Hawkins, and Frobisher, contributed their share to the explorations, and it was natural that reports of strange and wonderful lands and people, both real and exaggerated, should find their way back to England in Shakespeare's time. Caliban in part comes from these reports of exploration.

Prospero reproaches Caliban for having attempted to "violate the honour of my child," i.e., Caliban attempted to attack Miranda. Prospero, of course, having total power on the Island, could foil this attempt. He says that Caliban was ungrateful because he had been taught language by Prospero and repaid evil for good. Caliban replies that the island was his by inheritance and that Prospero had simply taken it from him by superior force and cunning. But Caliban recognizes, as we learn at the end of the dialogue between Prospero and his slave, that he has no choice but to obey, for he says of Prospero:

> His art is of such pow'r It would control my dam's god, Setebos, And make a vassal of him (lines 373–375).

The god Setebos does not appear in the play, but the name and quality of this being have some importance as showing how Caliban is initially ruled by the darkest superstition. Part of the action of *The Tempest* involves the education of Caliban as well as of most of the other characters. But Caliban, as a semihuman seriocomic character, has farthest to go in the matter of education.

The scene changes to another part of the Island to reveal the shipwrecked son of the King of Naples; he has just come ashore from the wreck and believes his father drowned. Hearing the strange music, including the famous song "Full fathom five thy father lies . . . ," Ferdinand is led by Ariel to a point where Prospero and Miranda meet him. Ferdinand realizes that he is in the midst of enchantment:

> This is no mortal business, nor no sound That the earth owes (lines 407–408).

Ferdinand is the first man, other than her father, whom Miranda has ever seen. She believes him to be a god or a spirit, but Prospero reassures her that he is a man, who has human senses and qualities. But Miranda artlessly gives her heart to Ferdinand almost from the moment she sees him. This is exactly what Prospero intends:

> It goes on, I see, As my soul prompts it (lines 419–420).

This statement by Prospero, spoken as an aside, is the first hint we have that everything that is to take place on the enchanted island, beginning with the meeting between Ferdinand and Miranda, which Prospero intends shall end in their marriage, is at the will of Prospero, who is in perfect control of everything and everybody—human, supernatural, and elemental—on the Island.

If Prospero intends Ferdinand to be his daughter's husband, one may reasonably observe that he does not show this in his initial treatment of Ferdinand. What is Prospero's motivation for his rough treatment of the young man who has already declared his wish to make Miranda the Queen of Naples?

Remember that Miranda herself is ignorant of men and of the world. She cannot, in order to be properly valued by her future husband, appear too easy a conquest. Ferdinand must win her, and Prospero intends that he do so by passing a kind of test. Therefore, he accuses Ferdinand of coming to the Island to spy, and in addition of being a usurper:

> Thou dost here usurp The name thou ow'st "ow'st" means "ownest"] not, and has put thyself Upon this island as a spy, to win it From me, the lord on't (lines 453–456).

Technically, Prospero would seem to be making up a story to test Ferdinand. On a deeper level Prospero's charge contains an element of truth. Ferdinand is a usurper. He is the son of a man who had assisted in the usurpation against Prospero. Usurpation—the act of taking away the power of a lawful King or Prince—was considered by the Elizabethans not only treason but blasphemy. The whole question of the powers and duties of a King or Prince is examined in this play. As you read the play, pay particular attention to the speeches on government and kingship, or the art of ruling well.

Ferdinand denies Prospero's charge that he is on the Island as a spy: "No, as I am a man!" (line 456). In this short phrase, another opposition or contrast is set up by implication: man against the beasts that are less than human and supernatural.

All of the qualities or kinds of beings opposite to man have slightly differing values. When Ferdinand calls himself a man, he is assigning to the word values not readily apparent. A man—a true one—cannot be a spy or a traitor.

Miranda tries to plead for Ferdinand:

Barnes & Noble, Inc.
1739 Olentangy River Road
Columbus, OH 43212
614-298-9516 05-31-01 502860 R003

William Shakespeare's [illegible] 3.95
0760710163

SUB TOTAL [illegible]
SALES TAX [illegible]
TOTAL 4.18
AMOUNT TENDERED
GIFT CARD REDEEM 4.18
Card #: 4490201588475
AUTH CODE: 0599079
BALANCE REMAINING 45.82

TOTAL PAYMENT 4.18
Thanks for shopping at Barnes & Noble!
#123677 05-31-01 07:29P

Booksellers since 1873

14 days with a receipt from any Barnes & Noble store.
Store Credit issued for new and unread books and unopened music after 14 days or without a sales receipt. Credit issued at lowest sale price.

Full refund issued for new and unread books and unopened music within 14 days with a receipt from any Barnes & Noble store.
Store Credit issued for new and unread books and unopened music after 14 days or without a sales receipt. Credit issued at lowest sale price.

Full refund issued for new and unread books and unopened music within

> There's nothing ill can dwell in such a temple. If the ill spirit have so fair a house, Good things will strive to dwell with't (lines 457–459).

But Prospero pretends to be hard and resists his daughter's pleas. He proposes to manacle Ferdinand and to make him do hard labor like a convict. When Miranda continues to intercede for Ferdinand, Prospero rebukes her:

> What, I say My foot my tutor? (lines 468–469).

That is, Miranda, his daughter, is subordinate to Prospero in all things; he can tell her what to do by the laws of relationship between parents and children. A relationship in which Miranda could tell him what to do would not be natural according to what the Elizabethans called the Law of Nature. Prospero prevents Ferdinand from resisting by placing a "charm" on him, which prevents him from moving at all. He says that Ferdinand is so possessed with guilt that he does not dare to strike with his sword. Prospero further says to Miranda that she has been deceived by Ferdinand's appearance only because she has never seen other men; that Ferdinand is inferior to most:

> To th'most of men this is a Caliban, And they to him are angels (lines 480–481).

Ferdinand has no choice but to give in and do what Prospero commands; he says in a brief soliloquy that he would sooner be imprisoned so long as he can see Miranda once a day than be free anywhere else in the world. To this, Prospero comments as an "aside" that "It works" (line 494). This means that the spell that Prospero has used—or rather, the "charm"—is working, as is the growing affection between Ferdinand and Miranda, which Prospero hopes will culminate in their marriage.

Ariel has been standing by, carrying out Prospero's commands, for he, Prospero, seems to work by the agency of his various servants. Prospero praises him and reminds him that if he does good work he shall be free. As the scene ends, Miranda speaks to Ferdinand, excusing her father's lack of hospitality to a shipwrecked guest. Prospero orders Ferdinand to follow along to the place where Prospero will put him to work, and once again, as the scene ends, cautions Miranda not to speak in behalf of Ferdinand.

COMMENT

The Tempest, with a total of 2,064 lines, is Shakespeare's second shortest play; only *The Comedy of Errors* is shorter. Thus the play must succeed in catching the audience right from the start. In this regard, the first scenes of *The Tempest* are outstandingly successful.

The first part of Act I, Scene 2, continues the exposition begun in Scene 1. The exposition is an explanation of what has occurred before the beginning of the action of the play: Its main purposes are to inform and to catch the audience's interest. If the exposition is successful, the audience or the reader is carried quickly into the action.

Telling the reader or audience what has happened in the past and is happening in the present is poor drama and not nearly as good a technique as showing or implying through action what has happened. Shakespeare is a great master of dramatic exposition. In *The Tempest* he surpasses himself.

It is necessary for Shakespeare not only to tell us the story of Alonso, Sebastian, Antonio, the shipwreck, Prospero, Miranda, Ariel, and Caliban; he must also in the first scenes of the play lead us to accept the illusion of enchantment and fantasy and magic in which the play is set. Therefore, he begins with a real event that his contemporaries would recognize: a shipwreck. From this, he leads us to the cell, the small room on the island where Prospero has his books and from which he controls the destinies of all the other characters. Prospero's power is a fantasy, but the point is that the difference between the real and the fantastic is so gradually shaded in that we are not aware of this difference. Shakespeare, in this scene, leads us to believe in the existence of the island on which Prospero exercises his magic, and this is of great importance to the effect of the play.

The action of the play begins at the time of the afternoon when an Elizabethan play would actually begin to be performed, and it will last until six, or the late afternoon, for Prospero's plan is that his work will be concluded by six.

The Tempest is the only Shakespeare play that observes the "unity of time." The tempest arises on the ship at two o'clock in the afternoon; by six o'clock everything is over. In contrast, the time period of *The Winter's Tale* is some seventeen years.

Though *The Tempest* is one of the most fantastic of Shakespeare's plays, Shakespeare, by his use of the most realistic time-scheme possible, helps us to suspend our disbelief in the strange nature of the events. In the course of the dialogue between Prospero and Ariel, we will learn other strange facts about this curious servant of Prospero.

In this scene is raised one of the key issues of *The Tempest*—the relationship among Prospero, Ariel, and Caliban. Each of the three characters is either less or more than a literal human being; they all have special qualities and powers that we accept as part of the machinery of the play. But what do these three characters, so closely related in action, mean? Most people viewing the play in the theater or reading it have concluded that they must have a meaning beyond the merely literal, and beyond the fact that all of them, especially Ariel and Caliban, are good entertainers.

Ariel gives an impression of lightness and lack of physical substance. He has many unusual qualities, which he uses in the service of his master, Prospero. The interchange between Prospero and Ariel, beginning at line 240 of this scene, is part of the exposition of Ariel's character. We learn that Ariel wishes his freedom; in this he is similar to Caliban, although in other respects he is quite different.

Several problems are raised about Prospero's character in the latter part of Act I, Scene 2. He is, or seems to be, open to criticism for his harsh treatment of Ariel, Caliban, and Ferdinand. In the case of Ferdinand, he makes a charge that he knows to be false. He accuses Ferdinand of being a spy on the Island and a traitor. Yet it is obvious that he plans that Ferdinand shall marry his daughter, Miranda—and he certainly would not want his daughter to marry a spy and traitor. If we allow this, Prospero then seems to "bear false witness against his neighbor." How can this be justified, especially since Prospero is supposed to be the wise, just, and benevolent ruler of everything on the enchanted island?

The answer lies in the action of *The Tempest,* which entails the education and initiation of all of the characters besides Prospero. From Caliban to Alonso to Miranda—all seem to develop and to learn more about the nature of reality during the course of the action.

All become educated in a higher sense. Prospero alone is unchanging, since he is already perfected at the beginning of the play. He is master of himself and can thus rule the others.

SUMMARY

In conclusion, we find that Act I, Scene 2 performs the following functions within the dramatic and intellectual structure of *The Tempest*:

1. The scene forms the major part of the exposition of the play.
2. It introduces us to Ariel, Caliban, and their master, Prospero, and establishes the complex relationship among these characters.
3. It is a transition scene between the matter-of-fact circumstances of "real life," as represented by the shipwreck in Act I, Scene 1, and the world of fantasy and symbolism represented by Prospero's cell and the enchanted island. Therefore, it leads us to suspend our disbelief and to accept the fantastic world in which the play occurs.
4. The plan of Prospero, involving the marriage of his daughter to the young Prince of Naples, Ferdinand, is revealed. We learn something further about the wisdom of Prospero when he determines to subject Ferdinand to a test to see if he is worthy to marry Miranda. At the same time, it is made quite clear that Prospero is in control of everything and foresees what will happen.
5. The concept of education is developed. All (except Prospero) must learn about their natures and what is required of them. Even Caliban learns.
6. The question of what constitutes a man is first raised in Ferdinand's reply to Prospero's charge that he is a traitor. Thus, whatever else the play is about; whatever may be said to be its theme, it is a play that in a profound way examines and analyzes the nature of man.

ACT II

ACT II: SCENE 1

The wordplay at the beginning of this scene helps to define further the various characters here. Gonzalo, the old courtier, counsels his king, Alonso, to be thankful for the escape from the shipwreck. This advice is in keeping with the cheerful and straightforward outlook manifested by Gonzalo in the brief first scene of Act I, where he combines philosophical-religious acceptance of what cannot be changed with a practical streak of self-help—suggesting that the passengers and crew of the apparently sinking ship can and should do all in their power to save themselves and the ship.

Every day sees newly ruined merchants and newly widowed sailor's wives as a result of the sea's wrath, says Gonzalo to his master. Therefore, Alonso should be thankful for his preservation, for

> few in millions Can speak like us. Then wisely, good sir, weigh, Our sorrow with our comfort (lines 7–9).

It is good fortune that any of the ship's passengers is still alive. But Alonso will not be comforted, because he believes his son, Ferdinand, to have been drowned. In the case of Alonso, the King of Naples, this is more than personal grief; his son was to have inherited the throne of Naples from him. Gonzalo, whose function it is to serve and counsel his master, advises moderation, as well as submission to what cannot be changed.

Sebastian and Antonio establish themselves in a few words as rather sarcastic and cynical individuals who mock Gonzalo rather cruelly, although the old man is defenseless against their taunts and largely ignores them. The two are intent on baiting Gonzalo, but they seem to be striking beyond him at the King himself in the wordplay at the beginning of Act II. Sebastian as the brother of Alonso has the right to speak more familiarly to the King than anyone else. Antonio is the brother of Prospero, the deposed Duke of Milan. At the beginning of the play Antonio is acting as the Duke of Milan, having usurped his brother's place as was recounted in the speech of Prospero to Miranda. Antonio has no idea that his brother is still alive and indeed is the supreme ruler over the enchanted island upon which Antonio has been cast.

There is a certain balance or similarity between the situation of Sebastian and that of Antonio—with the difference that while Antonio is the present Duke of Milan (having usurped his brother), Sebastian is simply a nobleman, the brother of Alonso. But it becomes clear that Sebastian wishes to depose and probably kill Alonso as Antonio had deposed and attempted to kill Prospero.

The intentions of Sebastian and Antonio, then, are identical. The speeches that subtly attack Alonso depend on wordplay. In line 18 Sebastian and Gonzalo make a play on the different words "dollar" and "dolour," or sadness. It seems cruel of Sebastian to make fun of Gonzalo's comforting speech, spoken to the King with perfectly good intention. Sebastian mocks the old man, picturing him as a sort of cheap entertainer who ought to be thrown a dollar's worth of coins for his efforts. Alonso keeps asking the old courtier to be silent, for his grief over the supposed death of Ferdinand is too great to be borne.

Of Gonzalo, Sebastian and Antonio say:

> Antonio: He misses not much. Sebastian: No; he doth but mistake the truth totally (lines 56–57).

This is because Gonzalo has been praising the island on which they have landed; he praises it as the means of their rescue and salvation:

> The air breathes upon us here most sweetly (line 45).

So Adrian says. Adrian is a neutral, and is thus the subject of attack by the cynical Sebastian and Antonio. The place is not good enough for them, they imply sneeringly, and this is their general attitude toward their surroundings. Therefore they think Gonzalo an old fool, as is Adrian judging from the cutting remarks they make.

In a deeper sense, Gonzalo is right. "He misses not much." He is in harmony with the spirit of the enchanted island, which is a healing and educative spirit, as we shall see later. Another thing that the "old fool" Gonzalo picks up more quickly than anyone else is that though all the men have been in a shipwreck, their garments are ". . . rather new-dyed than stained with salt water." (lines 62–63). Gonzalo is the first to perceive that the Island is a strange and enchanted place. His reaction is characteristic; he seems to accept his new circumstances cheerfully, just as he did the apparent sinking of the ship in the first scene of the play.

The subject of the marriage of Alonso's daughter, Claribel, to the King of Tunis is mentioned by Gonzalo. You will recall that the ship bearing the King of Naples home from the wedding of his daughter had been the one wrecked when the tempest sprang up suddenly. Therefore, it seems a bit rash for Gonzalo to refer to the marriage, for it simply reminds Alonso of his loss—both of his daughter, by marriage, and of his son, by drowning:

> Would I had never Married my daughter there! For, coming thence, My son is lost. . . . (lines 104–106).

Francisco, the other "neutral" character of the King's party, along with Adrian, reassures the King, in astonishingly vigorous poetic lines, that Ferdinand may still be alive, for he, Francisco, had seen Ferdinand strongly swimming toward the shore.

To Francisco's optimism about the fate of his son and heir, Alonso simply replies: "No, no, he's gone" (line 119). Alonso is a man bowed down by grief, and there is just a hint in this scene—confirmed later—that he is troubled by secret guilt. He may regard Ferdinand's supposed drowning as a just punishment inflicted because of his, Alonso's, offense in assisting Antonio to usurp Prospero's place as Duke of Milan. This may be the reason why Alonso seems prepared to believe the worst and to assume that the waves have taken his son and heir.

COMMENT

Act II, Scene 1, thus far helps establish the characters of the King of Naples and various members of his party:

1. Gonzalo appears optimistic, rather childlike and garrulous, but never offensive. He also proves himself to be quicker witted and more observant than the others when he perceives that although all of the people in his group have been in a violent storm and shipwreck, none shows any physical evidence of this.
2. The King of Naples, Alonso, is lost in his own grief over his son's supposed death. There is a suggestion, in line with the motif of guilt and punishment in *The Tempest*, that the King regards the death of Ferdinand as a judgment imposed on him for his complicity in the usurping of Prospero's throne.
3. Serious questions are raised about the qualities of character of Antonio and Sebastian.

The whole question of usurpation (the deposing of a lawful sovereign, whether by violence or by intrigue) was a burning one for Shakespeare's age. Some political theorists and religious writers went so far as to say that a King or Prince must never be deposed. A corollary was that a wicked tyrant should be borne by his people because in all probability he was the "Scourge of God"; i.e., a punishment sent by God for the sins of a nation or people.

The Tempest is in part about the characteristics of the just ruler as represented in the play by Prospero; it is also about the just counselor, represented by Gonzalo. Finally, the play concerns the relationship between the ruler and those whom he rules, as illustrated in Prospero's relationship toward all of the others on the island, especially to Ariel and Caliban, and also in Alonso's relationship to his subordinates, including the two potential murderers and traitors—Antonio and Sebastian.

Prospero and Alonso are contrasted in the play in terms of their adequacy as rulers according to the notions held by Shakespeare's age. Alonso is tainted by having connived at usurpation with Antonio. To the Elizabethan audience it would therefore come as no surprise to see Alonso's own life placed in danger—to see here a potential tragedy of usurpation and regicide (the murder of a King). Just as Alonso was guilty himself of complicity in such a crime, so Alonso himself may become a victim of it. This same theme—that once a lawful King is supplanted, there seems to be no end to the troubles of a country—is manifested also in Shakespeare's history plays, especially the great history plays *Richard II*, *Henry IV* Parts I and II, and *Henry V*.

During all of Queen Elizabeth I's long reign (1558–1603) there were plots against her throne, motivated by national and religious differences, for it was argued by some that as a daughter of Henry VIII by Anne Boleyn, Elizabeth had no lawful right to the throne and could justly be deposed, by force if necessary. Others saw this doctrine of the possible validity of usurpation as dangerous in the extreme since usurpation could lead to a civil war or a foreign invasion. We do not know Shakespeare's exact views on the subject, but as illustrated in many of the tragedies and history plays, his belief seems to have been that usurpation is always fraught with danger, and that once a ruler has been deposed no one can predict or control the outcome for the state. This is one of the ideas examined in *The Tempest* and why the play is one of Shakespeare's most philosophical dramas. It is in part a drama of political philosophy—a study of the use and abuse of power among rulers.

Prospero alone, on the enchanted island, has no superior exercising power over him and needs none.

Sebastian, Alonso's brother, reproaches Alonso, stating that he is sure Ferdinand has drowned, because of the King's stubbornness in marrying his daughter to an African, "Where she at least is banished from your eye . . ." (line 121). Sebastian actually seems quite bitter toward his brother as he rubs in the supposed loss of the heir, Ferdinand. As we shall see, Sebastian is not even sincere in this.

Gonzalo in the latter part of Scene 1 tries to be a peacemaker, to heal the grief caused by the missing Ferdinand; this explains the description of him as a surgeon.

Beginning with line 138, we have Gonzalo's famous "ideal commonwealth" speech, in which the old courtier explains what he would do if he had "plantation" of the island—i.e., if he could govern it without reference to other powers.

COMMENT

There is insufficient dramatic motivation for Gonzalo's speech concerning the ideal way of governing the island. It does not arise naturally out of the situation, except possibly from Gonzalo's wish to keep talking so that the King will forget his own grief. Gonzalo says that if he were setting up a little colony or state on the island, he would abolish all contractual relationships or relationships governed by law—in fact, he would abolish all laws, all forced labor, and all trade and go back to a primitive state of nature.

The state of nature, with no compulsion or law, would "insure" that the characters of all of the island's inhabitants would be pure and upright instinctively. Man would not be corrupted by trade and would do no work. There would be no crime, Gonzalo continues, on the island; this is an utterance loaded with ironic meaning, because the audience will shortly become aware, after Gonzalo's speech, that Sebastian and Antonio are bent on not only murder but treason and regicide, which were crimes worse than simple murder in the eyes of Shakespeare's contemporaries. For regicide and treason are crimes committed not against an individual so much as against the entire nation. Therefore, the state of innocence, which may admittedly be impractical, spoken about by Gonzalo in his speech, is still in the higher sense more "practical" than the destructive plotting engaged in by Sebastian and Antonio.

At the conclusion of the ideal commonwealth speech, Sebastian and Antonio, with their bitter tongues, shout "Long Live Gonzalo!" Alonso, too, asks his servant to keep quiet because the King would be alone with his grief. Gonzalo gently reproaches Sebastian and Antonio in line 176: "You would lift the moon out of her sphere. . . ." meaning that their boastful statements and their criticism of the King as well as of Gonzalo exceed their talents. This is exactly what Sebastian and Antonio plan to do: to upset the ordinary course of nature, symbolized by the cyclical movements of the moon, by committing treason and, in the case of Sebastian, fratricide (the murder of a brother).

COMMENT

Gonzalo's ideal commonwealth speech, poorly motivated dramatically, is taken at least in part from the essay "Of the Cannibales" by Michel de Montaigne (1533–1592), who wrote widely on many practical as well as speculative subjects. The essay referred to was translated by John Florio into English in 1603, so that Shakespeare could have read it prior to the composition of *The Tempest.* Further, there is a copy of Florio's translation of the essay in the British Museum which is thought perhaps to contain a genuine signature of Shakespeare, one of the few in existence. The signature's authenticity is not proved; if it is authentic, it would establish that Shakespeare had used the essay in *The Tempest.*

The tradition of an ideal state or commonwealth extends at least as far back as Plato's Republic. But the enchanted island is not a Utopia or ideal commonwealth. Shakespeare implies, in this play and in others, that humans are not capable of attaining directly the state of perfection in which they would exist in an ideal commonwealth. Humans must first be purified by trials and perhaps temptations and must above all come to know themselves. This Prospero achieves. Unlike Shakespeare's great tragic heroes, Prospero attains self-knowledge before there has been a tragic action.

> The situation all through *The Tempest* is potentially tragic, especially in view of the plot of Antonio, one worthy of an Iago. But it is only potential tragedy, for Prospero keeps control of all events.
>
> On the surface Gonzalo's famous speech seems to be irrelevant, and the King quite right in telling him to be silent, for he, Gonzalo, "dost talk nothing to me," says Alonso. On a deeper level of interpretation, the speech of Gonzalo does have meaning in terms of the play, as it relates to the problems of the governing of people which the play raises.
>
> The enchanted island is a place, indeterminate in space and time, which brings each being on it by the end of the play to see what he or she is—to learn. Only Prospero has attained self-knowledge before the beginning of the play. The island is a crucible in which various beings are tested.

Ariel enters (line 180) playing solemn music, while he is himself invisible. By means of a "spell," or more correctly, a "charm" (the difference is that a charm is the means appropriate to the kind of White Magic used by Prospero and his agents, in contrast to the spells used in Black Magic by such beings as Syrocax, mother of Caliban, who was a witch), Ariel affects all of the characters of the King's party except Alonso, Sebastian, and Antonio. Then Alonso falls asleep, leaving Sebastian and Antonio free to express unhindered their murderous intentions.

Note that Antonio, Prospero's brother, the usurping Duke of Milan, is the one who takes the lead and suggests that the two should murder Alonso. Antonio, who speaks rather convincingly to his more hesitant companion, offers reasons why they should murder the King: Ferdinand, the heir, is drowned; Claribel, the King's daughter, is in Tunis, "ten leagues beyond man's life" (line 241); she is so far away that even a letter can hardly reach her. Therefore, it would be likely that with Alonso out of the way Sebastian would succeed to the throne.

Sebastian remembers in turn that Antonio had been successful in getting rid of his own brother, Prospero, but he is still hesitant:

> But for your conscience (line 270).

Sebastian means that Antonio would be afraid to commit the act of violence against the King because his conscience would trouble him. But Antonio claims that he is not bound by conscience or abstract morality. The Good, for Antonio, is to seize power by whatever means, because power is good in itself.

As Sebastian and Antonio talk, and as Sebastian seems to be won over to the latter's plan of killing the King, Ariel suddenly sings in Gonzalo's ear:

> While you here do snoring lie, Open-eyed conspiracy His time doth take (lines 294–296).

Gonzalo wakes and immediately arouses the King, who wants to know why Sebastian and Antonio are "drawn"—i.e., have their swords unsheathed. The answer is obvious to the audience but not to the King or Gonzalo: the two conspirators have been surprised in the very attempt of taking Alonso's life. But neither has the brazenness to murder the King or his party while they are awake; Sebastian and Antonio are fit only to murder by stealth or to kill sleeping men. On the practical level, they would probably not succeed were the King awake, as it would be four against two.

Antonio and Sebastian make up a convenient lie, that they had heard the roaring of bulls and lions. The King may distrust them already: Who could know Sebastian better than his own brother? He turns to Gonzalo for corroboration of the story told by Antonio, and they are all put on guard. Gonzalo, too, may be a bit suspicious of the two secret conspirators. At the end of Scene 1, the party, swords drawn, sets off to explore the island and to see if Ferdinand can be found alive. Ariel, at the end of the Scene, having carried out the command of Prospero, goes back to report to his master.

COMMENT

The arch-villain of the play, according to the revelation of character that takes place in this scene, is Antonio. He is the opposite of Prospero, for as his brother is morally good, kindly, benevolent, and in command of himself, so Antonio is the victim of unscrupulous ambition for power, as he himself says. It is Antonio who helps further to corrupt Sebastian, and not the other way around. In line 218, when Sebastian says: "To ebb/ hereditary sloth instructs me," he also says something about his situation. As a younger son, Sebastian had been kept from the throne by Alonso, who had the rulership by inheritance. There is an implication that Sebastian is weak, that he does not take affirmative action, and that he can be easily led.

SUMMARY

Act II, Scene 1, then, has the following purposes:

1. Differentiation of the characters of Alonso, Sebastian, Antonio, and Gonzalo, and their further establishment as individuals necessary for the dramatic exposition;

2. The humor provided by the comic or seriocomic repartée between Gonzalo and Sebastian and Antonio. Critics have perceived that this scene is by no means successful as comedy, if comedy it is at all. Shakespeare seems to be dealing

with too serious a subject and writing on the edge of comedy, moving into the area of high philosophical drama.
3. Gonzalo is established in this scene as an admirable and alert subordinate and counselor to the King, utterly loyal to him, in contrast to the potential traitors and murderers. Gonzalo is not like Polonius in Hamlet; he is more like Kent, the courtier who upholds his king to the death in *King Lear*.
4. The plot against the life of Alonso is revealed in this scene, paralleling the plot against Prospero that we will see shortly.

ACT II: SCENE 2

Scene 2 begins with Caliban carrying firewood as he has been ordered to do by his master. He curses Prospero, asking his, Caliban's, gods to inflict on him horrible diseases. He also tells of the tortures his master inflicts on him for his rebellious thoughts. Sometimes spirits appear to him in the form of apes or snakes—animals that Shakespeare's contemporaries associated with magic and sorcery.

Trinculo, a jester, appears. His position at the court of Alonso, as the court jester, is to be a licensed Fool; thus, Trinculo has affinities with the Fool in *King Lear* and with similar characters in other Shakespeare plays. But Trinculo is presented as an ordinary man with the ability to make petty mischief. It is significant that initially Caliban worships him as a god, first believing that he is a Spirit sent by Prospero to torment him. Trinculo humorously and vividly describes the fantastic half-human creature Caliban. The beginning of Scene 2 does possess genuine humor, in contrast to the forced repartée of Sebastian and Antonio in the preceding scene; the humor occurs because of the incredulity with which Trinculo and then Stephano, drunk, view Caliban, and the comments they make about him. Stephano, a butler at the court of Alonso, enters unsteadily waving a bottle and singing a sea chanty.

COMMENT

The Jester, or Fool, of whom there are many examples in Shakespeare's comedies and tragedies, is a licensed entertainer at Court, permitted to say things with impunity that others, out of fear of punishment, would not say. He is more a cheap trickster than a magician or a minor oracle, at least in the case of Trinculo. But a Jester is often the source of witty sayings—something for the groundlings to laugh at—and Scene 2 provides such an opportunity. Scene 2 is also a drunk scene, and a drunk scene almost always gets a laugh. Humans in this situation in Shakespeare's plays sink to a level below that which is expected of them. The drunk scene, then, between Stephano, Trinculo, and Caliban, has a serious substratum, although it is very good entertainment.

Stephano and Trinculo, with the quickness of street rogues, understand that Caliban is more terrified of them than they are of him. Caliban, usually presented on stage dressed in a bearskin (because Trinculo describes him as a fish does not necessarily mean he looks like one; he can take a number of forms as presented in the actual theater), pleads with the two characters and arouses their curiosity. They quickly realize that they may be able to turn the situation to their own profit. They both show a low form of cunning in this. Neither knows whom Caliban is talking about when he refers to his torments at the hands of Prospero. Their reckless courage—especially that of Stephano—is in part the wine talking. Trinculo assumes that Caliban is a devil. Stephano (line 96) alludes to the proverb "He who sups with the Devil must needs have a long spoon," and he says with bravado that if Caliban is a devil and not a monster he will leave Caliban. But much of the "bravery" shown by the two rogues is clearly bravado. It will not stand any testing—and Stephano and Trinculo are, in a half-serious way, being tested as are Alonso and his party and even Ferdinand. This is not to say that Stephano and Trinculo are "serious" characters. They provide comic relief from the lofty and compressed action of *The Tempest.*

Initially the two are successful in fooling Caliban. Like Miranda, although at a primitive level, Caliban is an innocent: he has no experience of the "outside." Thus, in an aside to the audience, Caliban indicates that he thinks Stephano and Trinculo to be "fine" creatures. He decides that he will worship them as long as they do not turn out to be spirits sent by Prospero to torment him. The "celestial liquor" that Stephano brings is also a powerful inducement to Caliban.

Stephano tells Trinculo that he has a "whole butt" of the liquor (line 130); the butt, or cask, of wine has apparently been washed ashore after being heaved overboard by the sailors to lighten the King's ship, thought to be sinking at the beginning of the play. This fact is important for the future action because it is from "firewater" that Stephano, Trinculo, and Caliban will obtain sufficient courage to attempt to kill Prospero and take over the island.

Caliban seeks a new master, then, and finds him in the rather unadmirable person of Stephano:

> I'll fish for thee, and get thee wood enough. A plague upon the tyrant that I serve! I'll bear him no more sticks, but follow thee, Thou wondrous man! (lines 157–160).

Trinculo himself perceives that Caliban's trust is misplaced, as he observes that Caliban is a:

> . . . most ridiculous monster, to make a wonder of a poor drunkard! (line 162).

At the end of Scene 2 Caliban exits with his new master, singing somewhat unsteadily of his new-found "freedom":

> No more dams I'll make for fish, Nor fetch in firing At requiring, Nor scrape trenchering, nor wash dish. 'Ban, 'Ban, Ca-Caliban Has a new master. Get a new man. Freedom, high-day! high-day, freedom! freedom, high-day, freedom! (lines 175–182).

COMMENT

Shakespeare usually presents a serious meaning in a drunk scene, which is almost always good for comic effects as well. One remembers Cassio's famous remark, in Othello (Act II, Scene 3, lines 290–294), made after he has lost his military position as a result of a drunken brawl:

> . . . O God, that men should put an enemy in their mouths to steal away their brains! That we should, with joy, pleasance, revel, and applause, transform ourselves into beasts!

This is not to say that Shakespeare was writing a temperance tract or advising his audience to avoid strong drink. But in *The Tempest* a clear distinction is made between a human's rational and animal natures—as well as between the right exercise of rational faculties (represented by Prospero), and the perversion of these faculties (as indicated in the plot hatched by Antonio). At a comic level, we see humans (and half-humans, such as Caliban, who cannot really be expected to do any better) descending to the level and status of beasts. The comic effect of this scene is considerable in terms of the "roaring" drunkenness of Stephano and Trinculo. But the underlying seriousness of the distinction between rational human and human as beast should not be neglected. Ariel, an invisible and disembodied spirit, seems to lead these characters further astray through his magic later in Act III, but it must be kept in mind that Stephano and Trinculo have responsibility for their own actions. They are human beings who are degrading themselves.

SUMMARY

This short scene, Act II, Scene 2, has the following purposes:

1. It develops the plot in which Caliban has to kill his master, Prospero. This parallels the plot that Antonio formulates to kill his King.
2. It deepens the character sketch of the fantastic creature Caliban, who has a poetic view of reality, as shown by his speeches in this scene describing the enchanted island. Further, it shows Caliban's legitimate struggle to escape from bondage into freedom; this is made clear in the last lines of the scene. It appears sentimental to say that Shakespeare in the character of Caliban is protesting against the institution of slavery, for such protest did not come until more than a century later. Actually, Shakespeare treats Caliban's claim to freedom with skepticism: Caliban simply exchanges a beneficial relationship to his true master, Prospero, for a new servitude to two foolish knaves. The point is that in this scene Caliban becomes a being whom we may take seriously for what he represents.
3. It further distinguishes between Stephano and Trinculo. Stephano is the more aggressive of the two and bears the same relationship (as initiator of plots or as would-be ruler) to Trinculo that Antonio bears to Sebastian.
4. The scene points up a parallelism with the plot against Alonso's life, although the two plots are of unequal degrees of seriousness. For while the Stephano-Trinculo-Caliban plot against Prospero has many elements of comic relief, the same may not be said about the deadly serious plot of Antonio and Sebastian against Alonso.
5. Thus, one of the ultimate purposes of this scene is comic

relief from the plot against the King, the love affair of Ferdinand and Miranda, and the spells and charms of Prospero and his servants—all of which are presented in more or less serious terms.

ACT III

ACT III: SCENE 1

At the conclusion of the preceding scene, Caliban has been deceived into believing that Stephano and Trinculo, the lowest and most roguish members of the ship's company cast up on the enchanted island, are as gods; he has been led astray by his lack of experience of humankind.

At a much more elevated level, in the present scene we see a process of education taking place in which Miranda, who has been entirely innocent previously, now begins to learn more about the world, under the careful guidance of her father. Miranda's state and Caliban's are thus similar: both need at this point to learn more about the "outside world," to recognize various types of humans, good and bad. The scene, then, begins with Ferdinand; we see him undergoing his test. This scene, in other words, forms a continuity with Act I, Scene 2 at the end, where we saw Prospero leading Ferdinand out to do physical labor.

Ferdinand's task is to pile up thousands of heavy logs, and he must do this under Prospero's "sore injunction"—if he does not complete the work as he has been told to do, he will suffer for his neglect.

COMMENT

The best explanation of Ferdinand's soliloquy at the beginning of Act III seems to be that he is happy in doing his hard work, even though it is base work unworthy of a King's son and heir. But his thoughts are on Miranda, his beloved, whom he hopes to win as his Queen. So his labors are "refreshed" just by thinking about Miranda.

Miranda and Prospero enter; Miranda is visible to Ferdinand, while Prospero is invisible. Her language is characterized by startling figures of speech in keeping with the romantic tone of the scene: thus she says that the log that Ferdinand is lifting will regret the effort it caused him:

> When this burns, 'Twill weep for having wearied you (lines 18–19).

Ferdinand will not allow Miranda to help him with his task. It would dishonor him to do so, as she is the lady he serves. He is, in a sense, serving Miranda much as a knight would serve his lady. A certain amount of comedy arises from the incongruity of the situation at the beginning of this scene: the high-flown romantic language of Ferdinand, contrasted with his menial situation. But he is undergoing his test under the supervision of Prospero.

Prospero, unseen, contemplates the meeting of his daughter and his future son-in-law and is well satisfied. "Poor worm, thou art infected!" says Prospero of his daughter, but this is said in a tone of endearment. He means by this that Miranda has already fallen in love with the Prince, which is exactly Prospero's intention, both from his concern for the personal happiness of his daughter and for reasons of state. A line from the short English opera *Dido and Aeneas,* composed by Henry Purcell in 1689, perfectly reveals the source of the special concern a King or Prince would have for the contracting of such a marriage alliance:

> When monarchs unite, How happy their state, They triumph at once O'er their foes and their fate!

So it will be with Prospero, for he too will triumph over his foes when the marriage is contracted.

Ferdinand suddenly asks Miranda her name; he has been so enthralled by this beautiful creature that he never asked before. She answers even though her father had told her not to disclose who she is:

> . . . Miranda. O my father, I have broke your hest to say so! (lines 35–36).

The name "Miranda" means a female who is "one to be admired" (Latin). Ferdinand does, of course, "admire" her, addressing her as "admired Miranda" (line 37).

Ferdinand goes on in extravagant praise of Miranda while continuing to pile logs. Miranda tells him in turn (line 48) that she scarcely knows what other men and other women look like because she cannot remember her early childhood.

Ferdinand announces his "condition," or social status, to Miranda at this point, in lines closely involved with the political meaning of this scene. He is a prince, and since he believes that his father is dead, he thinks that he may have inherited the throne of Naples, although he wishes it were not so. This shows Ferdinand's soundness as both a son and a prince: he is not impatient for the throne, and he demonstrates true filial affection for his father.

By doing the menial work demanded of him, he feels that he "serves" his lady, and this excuses the kind of labor he must perform at Prospero's order:

> I am in my condition A prince, Miranda—I do think a king (I would not so!)—and would no more endure This wooden slavery than to suffer The fleshfly blow my mouth. Hear my soul speak! The very instant that

> I saw you did My heart fly to your service . . . (lines 61–66).

This is love at first sight between two royal persons who immediately recognize in each other their true mates.

Miranda asks artlessly: "Do you love me?" Normally, this is not a question that one in Miranda's position would ask, for natural innocence is, in the usual way of the world, obscured by guile and indirection. But Miranda is in a state of innocence on the enchanted island, quite removed from ordinary life, and therefore she does not have the devious ways one might expect such a beautiful woman to have in the world. Her lack of guile is charming rather than offensive.

Within a few lines, the couple have exchanged vows of fidelity and are engaged. A mutual promise to marry at some time in the future was, for the Elizabethans, a valid engagement. Prospero is pleased.

> Fair encounter Of two most rare affections! Heavens rain grace On that which breeds between 'em! (lines 73–75).

Prospero's observation can be understood in at least two senses. First, he signifies that he is pleased by the engagement, about which he has not been consulted, though he later ratifies it and gives the couple a proper betrothal.

Second, and more importantly, he sees "that which breeds between 'em" as not only affection, but ultimately progeny. To one of royal blood this was most important. Prospero's line will inherit another throne, that of Naples, in addition to the one already Prospero's by right: the throne of Milan.

Miranda does not force herself on Ferdinand as his wife; her directness is natural to one who has been brought up in isolation. But her royal qualities manifest themselves, as do Ferdinand's.

Prospero cannot rejoice at the event as much as the participants, but the engagement represents the success of one portion of his master plan. He leaves at the end of this scene, for he has much more to do before his plan can succeed entirely:

> I'll to my book; For yet ere supper time must I perform Much business appertaining. (lines 95–97).

COMMENT

This scene is relatively straightforward; it shows the success of one of Prospero's plans. At the beginning, Ferdinand is shown doing heavy manual labor under threat of dire punishment. But Ferdinand's status as an accused traitor and spy rapidly changes in this scene to that of the betrothed of Miranda and the future King of Naples, as well as the son-in-law-to-be of Prospero.

Again, Prospero is established as the character who is in control of everything and everybody on the Island. At hidden levels of symbolism and suggestion, it is made clear by hints in the play that nothing can go wrong with Prospero's plans; he is omniscient and omnipotent with respect to the other beings on the Island. At the same time, suspense must be maintained dramatically, and Shakespeare does this by a combination of the Sebastian-Antonio plot against the King and the Stephano-Trinculo-Caliban comic and drunken conspiracy against Prospero. Neither has the slightest chance of success. This scene of the betrothal of Ferdinand and Miranda represents a change in the action, then, as it is the resolution of the first thread of Prospero's complex plan, which involves the further "education" of everyone on the Island, including his daughter. The scene is an idyll, or romantic interlude. It suggests more than it states, and what it suggests, along with its romantic atmosphere created by the engagement of the lovers without any of the usual artifices and denials, is the great power of Prospero to dispose the affairs of others to a good end.

SUMMARY

Act III, Scene 1, has these purposes:

1. The transition of Ferdinand from a suspected traitor and spy undergoing punishment to the status of Miranda's betrothed husband.
2. The completion of one phase of Prospero's plan; this occurs with the engagement of his daughter, his heir, to the heir of the King of Naples, which will strengthen Prospero's dynastic prospects, a very important consideration for Shakespeare's world.
3. The further characterization of the innocent and unaffected pair, Ferdinand and Miranda, who are presented as natural aristocrats. Their royal blood would manifest itself no matter how humble the surroundings, as demonstrated in this scene.

ACT III: SCENE 2

On another part of the island, Caliban, Stephano, and Trinculo are wildly drunk; this is a continuation of Act II, Scene 2. The reader should note how the stories of Ferdinand and Miranda, the most ideal, innocent, and attractive types of man and woman, are alternated and contrasted with the comic relief provided by the drunken Stephano and Trinculo and the wild man or man-beast Caliban. The two humans who are descending to the level of beasts, along with Caliban, are found at the beginning of this scene drinking from Stephano's butt of wine.

Caliban has taken Stephano as his lord and master; he asks if he may lick Stephano's shoe and asserts that he will not serve Trinculo, for "he is not valiant." Trinculo mocks Caliban as a "deboshed fish." Caliban, offended, asks protection of his lord:

> Lo, how he mocks me! Wilt thou let him, my lord? (line 29).

In the above line, "let" means "stop."

Then, in line 30, Shakespeare makes a play on the meaning of *natural. Natural* means "according to nature," or, in the case of Caliban, a "natural" being without any spirit or soul—merely a part of nature. *Natural* as a noun means one who is an idiot or imbecile, a fool. But Caliban turns out to be more intelligent and more "human" than either of his two companions, so in this sense he proves himself to be not a "natural." A monster is by definition unnatural, so this is a play on words—the kind of play on words in which Trinculo and Stephano, as well as Antonio and Sebastian, engage. It may be significant that Prospero, the lord and master of the island, does not engage in wordplay; what he says is what he means, if his hearers can understand his message. For most of the other characters, words can have various serious and comic meanings that are less than straightforward, to fit in with the character of the speaker.

Stephano drunkenly threatens Trinculo, telling him to be respectful of his betters. There is a suggestion that even in a "state of nature," where humans exist without laws or governments, a natural authority or chain of leadership will be established; if there are even two humans, one will become the master. This is an implied critique of Gonzalo's ideal commonwealth speech of Act II, Scene 1.

Ariel appears at this point, maintaining invisibility by magic arts, just as Caliban says to his new master:

> As I told thee before, I am subject to a tyrant, A sorcerer, that by his cunning hath cheated Me of the island (lines 40–42).

Ariel says to Caliban aloud: "Thou liest." Shakespeare uses this scene for comic relief—while Ariel is invisible, his voice can be heard by the drunken pair as well as by Caliban. Stephano believes that it is Trinculo who says, "Thou liest." Accusing Trinculo of giving him the lie, he strikes him. In Shakespeare's time, for one gentleman to accuse another of calling him a liar was grounds for a duel. Here Stephano and Trinculo are aping their betters, for both act as though they were kings and noblemen instead of ordinary rogues. They are examples of men acting under no restraint of lawful authority.

Ariel, then, says three times that Caliban has lied. The third time, Stephano mistakenly beats Trinculo for having said that he, Stephano, has lied.

COMMENT

This scene, too, is very humorous, since Stephano and Trinculo are reeling around the stage drunk. Part of the humor arises from the two rogues' pretending to be noblemen, with Stephano giving orders as though he is the feudal lord of Caliban. The serious undertones of this scene emerge because it is Caliban who seems more in control of himself, more single-minded in what the three should do to wrest control from Prospero, than the two humans. Though a monster, a beast, he behaves more according to the dictates of reason than the others, and thus he becomes more of a serious character. The monster evolves in the direction of humanity while the two men sink further toward the level of the beast.

Caliban proposes to his would-be master a means whereby they can destroy Prospero and then attain the rulership of the island.

> . . . thou mayst brain him, Having first seized his books, or with a log Batter his skull, or paunch him with a stake, Or cut his wesand [windpipe] with a knife (lines 85–88).

The books are the key, Caliban says. Without them, "he's but a sot, as I am." This statement happens to be false, for as Prospero's power originates in his own character, of which the books, the magical charms, and the troop of Spirits who serve him are a symbolic manifestation.

Caliban then tells his new "master" about Miranda, and Stephano decides that he will make her his queen and together they will rule the island. He vows to kill Prospero and to take Miranda by force, as well as to make Trinculo and Caliban "viceroys" on the island. Finally, he apologizes for beating Trinculo.

Suspense is thus built up to a higher pitch as this plot against Prospero's life is advanced. Ariel, who has been listening in, still invisible, says that he will inform his master.

Even though Ariel goes through the motions of keeping his master informed, we somehow get the idea that Prospero already knows everything—that he does not even need Ariel's assistance, although he makes Ariel think that he does. He is educating Ariel, too, in service, as he is educating in different ways everyone on the island.

Ariel reenters playing a tune on a tabor and pipe, or small drum and fife. Stephano and Trinculo, even through the fog of liquor, are terrified at the supernatural music because they can see nobody playing. Even here, there is a distinction between Stephano and Trinculo, for Stephano defies the unseen powers:

> If thou beest a man, show thyself in thy likeness. If thou beest a devil, tak't as thou list (lines 124–125).

Caliban begins to test his new master when he asks him,

> Art thou afeard?

Stephano replies that he is not afraid; this bravado is in contrast to the reaction of Trinculo, which is to pray for deliverance while utterly terrified.

Another of the many speeches of almost supernaturally beautiful poetry occurs in the latter part of this scene. As in the case of the other such speeches, e.g., Prospero's speech, "Our revels now are ended . . ." (Act IV, Scene 1), the description of the enchanted island by Caliban is insufficiently motivated dramatically. Shakespeare effortlessly creates these lines from an excess of power and creativity:

Be not afeard. The isle is full of noises, Sounds and sweet airs that give delight and hurt not. Sometimes a thousand twangling instruments Will hum about mine ears; and sometimes voices That, if I then had waked after long sleep, Will make me sleep again; and then, in dreaming, The clouds methought would open and show riches Ready to drop upon me, that, when I waked, I cried to dream again (lines 132–139).

These lines characterize Caliban as a natural apprehender of beauty, despite his misshapen form. In fact, he speaks some of the most beautiful poetry in the play.

COMMENT

The above speech illustrates the sound imagery, or appeal to senses other than the visual, found in *The Tempest.* Professor Caroline Spurgeon, in a pioneering study of Shakespeare's imagery, pointed out that in *The Tempest* "it is the sense of sound which is thus emphasized, for the play itself is an absolute symphony of sound, and it is through sound that its contrasts and movement are expressed, from the clashing discords of the opening to the serene harmony of the close." This point is quite relevant here as this speech is one of the outstanding examples of the auditory imagery in the play and is rather incongruously set in a scene that exists to provide comic relief. Yet the words and images spoken by Caliban are magical in their evocative power. Further, the musical and sound imagery points out again one of the major oppositions in the play, which may be expressed as:

Order versus Disorder, or Harmony versus Disharmony

Caliban keeps urging that Prospero must be destroyed; he is still desperate to escape the domination, or what he considers to be the domination, of his old master. As the scene ends, Stephano, Trinculo, and Caliban move off stage to the music that Ariel plays to lure them along.

SUMMARY

The purposes of Act III, Scene 2, are:

1. Comic relief.
2. The continued building up of suspense, especially in terms of the plot against the life of Prospero.
3. The further establishment of the interesting and not altogether unattractive character of Caliban, as he transfers his allegiance from Prospero to Stephano.

ACT III: SCENE 3

As Stephano, Trinculo, and Caliban go crashing off through the woods, we find the party of the King wandering about on another part of the island. We know that this party too—certainly Sebastian and Antoni—represents the deterioration of human kind rather than its perfection. They plot murder and treason against their king, just as Caliban and his cohorts plot against Prospero.

Gonzalo and Alonso are, in the beginning of Scene 3, tired and disheartened. Alonso's spirit is dull, for the King is now certain that his son is drowned. Antonio, again, viciously whispers in Sebastian's ear to the effect that "he's so out of hope" that it makes Antonio glad—a most unnatural statement:

> I am right glad that he's so out of hope (line 11).

Antonio means by this that since the King is so beaten down by sorrow for his lost son, he will be even easier to kill. But while this makes even clearer the picture of Antonio as the instigator of the plot, and a most cold-blooded villain, it still shows that neither Antonio nor Sebastian possesses the ruthlessness necessary to confront the King while he is awake in order to kill him. If either of them did have such courage, *The Tempest* would then have been a tragedy, not a tragicomedy or dramatic romance. Sebastian and Antonio agree to effect their plot that same night. Suddenly, as they have concluded their agreement once again, there is strange music. Prospero appears. In the theater, he would stand on an upper stage, invisible to the members of the King's party. He directs various strange shapes, who bring in a banquet and dance about it, inviting the famished king and his companions to eat.

COMMENT

The feast, with the dance, is entertainment—another interlude in the midst of the serious business as the plot moves toward its climax. In terms of the allegorical dimensions of the play, it further shows Prospero's power. Magicians were noted for conjuring up illusory banquets, but there is a deeper allegory here: a temptation scene, or a banquet with overtones of sacrament and religious ritual. Sebastian and his companions are unfit to partake of the banquet, for they are, as Ariel is to say in his long speech as he appears to them, "three men of sin."

Fabulous monsters are mentioned by the members of the King's party as they contemplate the banquet with hungry eyes. These include the unicorn, which has only one horn; and the phoenix, which regenerates itself periodically on its own funeral pyre and was the subject of much mythological interpretation in the Middle Ages and in Shakespeare's age. The King and his companions are amazed; they realize what Gonzalo, the supposedly obtuse old courtier, has long since known: that a supernatural agency is at work on the island. Gonzalo stands his ground, which is another piece of evidence that we should accept him as a kindly and wise old man rather than as a garrulous fool. He points out that the harpies and strange shapes have very gentle manners as they go about setting the banquet:

> For certes these are people of the island, Who, though they are of monstrous shape, yet, note, Their manners are more gentle-kind than of Our human generation you shall find Many—nay almost any (lines 30–34).

Prospero comments on this, from his perch of invisibility:

> Honest lord, Thou hast said well; for some of you there present Are worse than devils (lines 35–37).

He refers to those who had a part in deposing him from his dukedom, as well as to the plotters who seek the life of the King. After further talk about the wonders of the little-known paths of the world, the party determines to taste the banquet. Alonso himself realizes that this may be a trap and that the banquet may be poisoned, but he is indifferent, "since I feel/ The best is past" (lines 50–51). By this he means that he has little wish to live, so great is his sense of loss regarding his son.

As the characters begin the banquet, Ariel appears dressed like a harpy (a mythical creature possessing the face and body of a woman and the wings and claws of a bird), accompanied by thunder and lightning. Clapping his wings upon the table, he makes the banquet vanish with a "quaint device," or a trick of the stage.

COMMENT

There is an element here of temptation, with some religious overtones involving sin or guilt and their punishment. This is pointed out in Ariel's long speech, one of the more famous passages in the play, whose meaning has been much debated. The speech of Ariel is really an accusation, a bill of particulars, a kind of grand jury indictment of the "three men of sin." Note that the entire speech is directed only at the three: Alonso, Antonio, and Sebastian:

You are three men of sin, whom destiny—That hath to instrument this lower world And what is in't—the never-surfeited sea Hath caus'd to belch up you; and on this island, Where man doth not inhabit, you 'mongst men Being most unfit to live . . . (lines 53–58).

This implies that the members of the party are outcasts from humanity, having forfeited their status as human beings by some crime that places them outside Nature, so that even the "never-surfeited sea" rejects them. Destiny has "to instrument" this lower world. This means simply that the impersonal force or power of Destiny has the earth as its instrument.

It is thus implied in this speech that there is both a lower or actual material world and a higher or ideal world—a Platonic notion familiar to Shakespeare and his contemporaries. By plotting murder, usurpation, and fratricide as well as treason, the members of the King's party have conformed not to the ideal but rather to the most brutal aspects of the lower world. They have incurred guilt, which must be purged and purified. Thus Alonso, Sebastian, and Antonio are also being tested and tried, even as was Ferdinand, though in the latter case his testing was briefer and less harsh.

Both Alonso and Sebastian draw their swords at this point. Ariel mocks them for doing so:

> You fools! I and my fellows Are ministers of Fate. . . . (lines 60–61).

They have no material substance. How, then, can Ariel and his agents be hurt by the swords? Ariel casts here, by Prospero's power, a charm on the guilty men so that even if they could use the swords they are now unable to lift them. Ariel, at this point, recounts the crimes, primarily centering around the charge that the three

> From Milan did supplant good Prospero (line 70).

Here the loss of Ferdinand is tied up with the punishment for usurpation, as it has been earlier in the play. Alonso now knows what his guilt is, though he has sensed it earlier. During the time while Ariel is speaking, the party appears paralyzed, as if in a trance.

The grammatical structure of this whole speech is complicated, but it means that Ariel, as one of the ministers of fate, is called upon to be an avenger of Prospero, and that the fates have pronounced on the three "lingering perdition," meaning that the characters must undergo a purgation of their guilt leading to "a clear life ensuing"—a life free of guilt. At this point we are doubly sure that the play has as one of its important themes purgation and purification from guilt.

In the final portion of Scene 3, Ariel vanishes to the accompaniment of praise for him and his performance from his hidden master, who sees all. The shapes put on a dance with comic overtones: perhaps mocking the hungry men further as they remove the table on which the feast had been set.

Now Prospero has his enemies where he wants them; as he says:

> My high charms work, And these, mine enemies, are all knit up In their distractions. They are now in my pow'r . . . (lines 88–90).

But it has been clear from the action of the play that Prospero has been in control of his enemies from the very beginning, when the ship was caught in the magical tempest. Prospero then leaves to visit his daughter and prospective son-in-law.

Alonso, staring, still partly in a trance, seems to think that the thunder has spoken to him, for Prospero appears as a vision.

> . . . the thunder That deep and dreadful organ pipe, pronounced The name of Prosper; it did bass my tres-

> pass. Therefore my son i'th' ooze is bedded . . . (lines 97–100).

The correlation between Alonso's sin against Prospero and the drowning, or supposed drowning, of Ferdinand, has been made earlier in the play in Alonso's mind: he has a conscience and knows he has done wrong and must be punished for the wrong. Alonso is reminded of his guilt. He is so overcome with remorse that he no longer wishes to live; he would prefer to join Ferdinand.

Alonso is suicidal, while Sebastian and Antonio, more deeply marked with guilt since they plan a murder, swear to fight all the "legions of fiends" as they exit in a frenzy of fear and defiance. Gonzalo speaks the final and most significant lines as the scene ends:

> All three of them are desperate. Their great guilt, Like poison given to work a great time after, Now gins to bite the spirits (lines 106–108).

This is the first time that Gonzalo has even hinted at all he knows about the guilt of the three, but obviously he knows what they have done to Prospero. Remember that at the beginning of the play Prospero had mentioned that it was Gonzalo who provided the means to save his life and the life of Miranda. So it is clear that Gonzalo knows much yet forgives much.

COMMENT

Gonzalo has a parallel with the faithful and noble servant Kent, the follower who continues to safeguard and watch over King Lear even while the King in his anger banishes him. Gonzalo likewise will look after the best interests of his master, Alonso, and follows the distracted three along with Adrian and Francisco, to see that they do not harm themselves or others. With this high point of spiritual tension the scene ends.

SUMMARY

The purposes of Act III, Scene 3 are:

1. To indicate guilt and the realization of guilt in the persons of Alonso, Sebastian, and Antonio.
2. To further advance the plot against Alonso's life and the counterplot or counterintrigue involving Prospero's plan to punish those who had dealt with him unjustly.
3. To illustrate the power of Prospero and present it in a way that would be appealing to the audience of Shakespeare's day, e.g., the dances of the strange Shapes and the antics of the harpy, Ariel.
4. To present a philosophical, hierarchical view of the universe and of nature, with division into the ideal higher world and the more material and gross lower world.
5. To signal the beginning of the process of repentance and purification on the part of the King and of his guilty companions. The King is a man who is at this point mortally conscience stricken, believing that his son has died as a result of his own transgression.

ACT IV

ACT IV: SCENE 1

At the beginning of this scene Prospero abandons the stern posture that he has taken toward Ferdinand, who has successfully undergone his period of trial and testing. His trial, incidentally, is very mild compared to those undergone by all of the other guilty characters on the Island. This points up the fact that Ferdinand has been almost guiltless; he is in every way a model young man, son, and prince, and such guilt as he may have stems from his inheritance. He is, after all, the son of a King who has participated in usurpation, and in the King's guilt Ferdinand shares by birth, but not by his own actions or inclinations. Therefore his punishment is physical only:

> . . . all thy vexations Were but my trials of thy love, and thou Hast strangely stood the test: here, afore Heaven, I ratify this my rich gift (lines 5–8).

Ferdinand here explicitly learns from Prospero that he has been subjected to a test, and that in Prospero's view he has passed it as a King's son should. ("Strangely" had, in Elizabethan times, the meaning of "care; respectful attention.") We have seen Ferdinand resisting the imposition of the menial task at first, until he was forced to do the work by Prospero's charm. He then gladly accepted the heavy physical burdens as he convinced himself that all was in the service of his lady. Such a belief on Ferdinand's part was in keeping with the aristocratic code by which Shakespeare's audience expected a king's son to behave.

Prospero, then, ratifies the gift very formally: "a third of mine own life," which probably means that Prospero has devoted himself to Miranda's upbringing for a third of his 45 years (by the chronology of the play). Prospero does not have any children other than Miranda.

The betrothal of Ferdinand and Miranda is made formally. Prospero emphasizes several times the necessity for the religious rites and ceremonies, the "full and holy rite" (line 17). Ferdinand and Miranda are enjoined not to consider themselves as having the rights of married persons until they undergo the marriage ceremony. Ferdinand swears not to anticipate the delights of his wedding day, whereupon Prospero praises him further and summons his chief lieutenant, Ariel. Ariel is to provide an entertainment for Prospero, Ferdinand, and Miranda, and Prospero orders him to go and bring the "rabble" over whom he has power. These would be inferior Spirits whom Prospero can command by his white magic.

While Ariel goes to do Prospero's bidding, the master of the Island once again warns Ferdinand that he and his bride must preserve chastity until their marriage.

COMMENT

Prospero's emphasis on chastity has struck some critics as out of keeping with the forgiving and reconciliatory spirit manifested by him as the play develops. The dwelling on the subject had both a comic and a serious purpose. Wedding night jokes—especially about the bridegroom as he approaches marriage and its consummation—appealed to Shakespeare's audience much as they do to a modern audience. This is the comic aspect of the marriage.

There is a more profound aspect of Prospero's insistence on chastity. *The Tempest* is a drama of moral as well as political philosophy; in the sphere of Elizabethan ethics and morality, it sets up the opposition between human reason and lower passions. Much of the action of the play revolves around the idea that some of the characters cast up on the enchanted island must undergo a kind of ritual purification for past guilt that they have incurred. A state of chastity may symbolize the state of purity to be attained by these characters. Also present here is the theological concept that virginity is a more excellent state than matrimony. Although the latter is an "honorable estate," it must be entered into with prescribed rites.

Beginning with line 60, the masque presented by Ariel for the amusement of his master is acted. Iris, or a Spirit representing her, begins the entertainment. Iris is a personification of the rainbow and a messenger of the gods. She addresses

Ceres, the protectress of agriculture and also the goddess of fertility. The poetry of the speech of Iris should not be overlooked as it conjures up a picture of bounty:

> Of wheat, rye, barley, vetches, oats, and pease; Thy turfy mountains, where live nibbling sheep, And flat meads thatch'd with stover, them to keep; Thy banks with pioned and twilled brims, Which spongy April at thy hest betrims, To make cold nymphs chaste crowns. . . . (lines 60–66).

At the end of this speech, Juno descends. Juno was not only queen of the gods but the patroness of childbirth and the protectress of women about to give birth.

Ceres has been summoned "a contract of true love to celebrate." Her speech is critical of Venus and her son Cupid because of the theft of the daughter of Ceres, Proserpina, as a result of Cupid's machinations.

The climax of this masque, making splendid the austere cell of Prospero, occurs as Juno and Ceres impart a marriage blessing to Ferdinand and Miranda. Prospero explains, in answer to Ferdinand's question, that the performers are:

> Spirits, which by mine Art I have from their confines call'd to enact My present fancies (lines 120–122).

Ferdinand's answer is significant:

> Let me live here ever; So rare a wonder'd father and a wise Makes this place Paradise.

The Nymphs enter and continue to celebrate the marriage, accompanied by Reapers. Suddenly, Prospero remembers something: the plot of Caliban and the two drunkards against his life. He dismisses the Spirits rather abruptly and seems distracted and "in some passion," as Ferdinand observes. In fact, his daughter says that never yet has she seen him so angry. The Spirits vanish in a "strange, hollow and confused noise." At this point Prospero begins what is certainly the most famous speech in the play, and one of the best-loved pieces in all of Shakespeare's work.

COMMENT

The masque contains more thematic implications than one might suppose. At first glance, the appearance and singing and dancing of the Spirits, traditionally dressed in rich and colorful costumes, seems just an interlude. But it harmonizes completely with the healing and regenerative aspects of the enchanted island and of its master, Prospero, who indeed promotes "Earth's increase, foison [abundance] plenty."

Prospero realizes that the plot of Caliban has reached a critical point. Actually, this is an illusory statement, for Prospero has known all along what would happen and is at no time in any danger from the plot. Even his anger at the presumption of his slave in daring to plot against him seems not quite real and not sufficiently motivated dramatically.

Speaking of dramatic motivation, Prospero's famous speech seems hardly motivated at all; it simply proceeds out of an excess of creative power on the part of the supreme English poet. But the question is: what is the special magic of these lines:

> You do look, my son, in a moved sort, As if you were dismayed. Be cheerful, sir. Our revels now are ended. These our actors, As I foretold you, were all spirits and Are melted into air, into thin air; And, like the baseless fabric of this vision, The cloud-capped towers, the gorgeous palaces, The solemn temples, the great globe itself, Yea, all which it inherit, shall dissolve, And, like

> this insubstantial pageant faded, Leave not a rack behind. We are such stuff As dreams are made on, and our little life Is rounded with a sleep (lines 146–158).

This speech asserts that life is a dream and that humans are of little more substance than the Spirits who have so casually been called up for a few minutes of entertainment and who have so quickly vanished. As a work of genius, the speech defies analysis. The ideas expressed in it are commonplace Elizabethan notions: that a human's material life is not quite real, and that life may be described as a dream or a moment's interlude between the realities of birth and death—"the dreamcrossed twilight between birth and dying," as T. S. Eliot put in it in our own century. The evanescence of earthly things is an orthodox Christian idea: that at the Last Judgment the material world will come to an end. Sermons on this topic were familiar to the audience that saw *The Tempest*, and yet such sermons survive, if at all, in obscurity. Prospero's speech will outlast any sermon.

COMMENT

The speech may also serve as an implied corrective and counterbalance to the delight in the sheer physical world which permeates the play. Even Caliban describes the enchanted island, in its physical aspects, as a delightful place, as in his speech in Act III, Scene 2: "the isle is full of noises/ Sounds and sweet airs. . . ." But the religious temper of Shakespeare's time involved at least formal subscription to the idea that everything in the physical world is vanity and will ultimately pass away: that spiritual things alone are real and unchanging. Therefore, Prospero's speech contributes to the balance in the play between:

1. Body and Spirit
2. The Created World and The World of Eternal Spirit.
3. Natural Fact and Supernatural Reality

The notion that Prospero had "almost forgotten" the plot against his life is maintained. Prospero calls Ariel to him in order to arrange to foil Caliban's plot and to punish the human monster and his two drunken associates. As Ariel describes his actions, it seems that he has led on the plotters, who have all sunk to the level of beasts:

> So I charmed their ears That calf-like they my lowing followed through . . . (lines 178–179).

The three have been led by Ariel until they have found themselves in the "filthy mantled" pool of stagnant water near Prospero's cell. At this point Prospero orders Ariel to bring various brightly colored clothes for "stale" [a decoy] to catch the prospective thieves and murderers.

Prospero again denounces Caliban as a "devil, a born devil," who can only be trained, or rather restrained and chastised, by hard punishment. But an interesting aspect of this scene, related to the thematic content of the play, is that Caliban's punishment, as it turns out, is astonishingly light.

COMMENT

Prospero reflects a characteristic idea of Shakespeare's age when he observes of Caliban:

> And as with age his body uglier grows, So his mind cankers (lines 191–192).

In other words, the moral condition of the soul is reflected in one's beauty or deformity of body, and vice versa: body and soul have a close relation, and ugliness of soul is often reflected in ugliness of body. Shakespeare uses this idea in *Richard III.*

As the three plotters approach the cell, Prospero and Ariel remain invisible, watching them. Suddenly they see the sort of clothesline upon which Ariel has hung the glistening apparel.

Caliban, showing more wisdom than his two sodden masters, tries to get them to proceed with the plot and not to be distracted by such "trash."

> Let it alone, thou fool! It is but trash (line 223).

At this point, Caliban himself is beginning to realize that he has worshipped a fool and a dullard, for Trinculo and then Stephano are easily distracted from the plot in order to attempt to steal the clothing. Just as they are seizing the flimsy appearances of garments Spirits appear in the shapes of dogs and hounds, with Prospero and Ariel setting them on. Prospero orders that his "goblins" grind the joints of the plotters and rack them with cramps and convulsions. The three run off, roaring with pain, while Prospero observes that all of his plans have come to fruition on schedule. As Act IV ends, Prospero, speaking to Ariel—even more so to himself—summarizes the state of the action when he says:

> At this hour Lie at my mercy all mine enemies. Shortly shall all my labors end, and thou Shalt have the air at freedom. For a little, Follow, and do me service (lines 261–265).

COMMENT

Note the difference in quality between the punishment Prospero inflicts on the three guilty noblemen, Alonso, Sebastian, and Antonio, and that which he inflicts on the three plotters who provide the comic relief of the play, Stephano, Trinculo, and Caliban.

The torments of the three nobles are spiritual and psychological. The three "men of sin" are told their offenses by Ariel at the end of Act III, Scene 3, and all of them become desperate. Gonzalo accompanies them with Adrian, to watch over them so that in their remorse they will not do violence to themselves or to others. Their crimes among the worst of which Shakespeare's age could conceive—attempted murder, regicide, fratricide, and usurpation against a lawful ruler, or treason. The situation is fraught with potential tragedy, and if it were not for Prospero, the plots and actions of the three men would result in the catastrophic kind of tragedy found in *Hamlet*, *King Lear*, *Othello*, and *Macbeth*. Antonio has been likened in his unscrupulousness to Iago, the villain of *Othello*. He could do an immense amount of mischief were he not restrained by Prospero.

The three are spiritually tormented, in part by their own guilt, in part by the charm of Prospero. The King, Alonso, suffers the heaviest punishment, because in addition to the punishments inflicted by Prospero directly, the King also believes that his son and heir has been drowned. This is the worst torment of all for him, because it means that the dynasty of Naples would come to an end. This was the great fear of any Renaissance ruler: that his line would end. This fear was much on the minds of the English during the reign of Queen Elizabeth I (1558–1603) and after, when the line of succession to the English throne was unsettled.

On the other hand, Trinculo, Stephano, and Caliban have been guilty only of a comic plot against Prospero and of the attempted theft of a few trashy clothes, as well as of the venial offense of drunkenness. They—or at least the two humans—have reduced themselves to the level of beasts and are treated as such by Prospero when he sets the dogs on them just as one might do to a bear or other vicious animal. Their punishment is physical, not mental or spiritual, and therefore much lighter than the torment suffered by the three noblemen.

The contrast between the forms of punishment should be kept in mind. Further, note that the purpose of the punishment, on Prospero's part, is not only correction but also education. Those who benefit the most from Prospero's lessons are, strangely enough, at opposite ends of the human social chain or power structure: the King, Alonso, and the subhuman monster, Caliban.

SUMMARY

Act IV, which is not further divided into scenes, ends on a note of triumph for Prospero, as he has punished his two sets of enemies and arranged the marriage between his daughter and the Prince of Naples, Ferdinand, thus ensuring his own line of succession in Milan.

Act IV accomplishes the following:

1. It brings the testing of Ferdinand to a conclusion, further developing his character and demonstrating that he is fit to be the son-in-law of Prospero.
2. It concludes the formal betrothal of Ferdinand and Miranda.
3. It provides the semicomic masque of Juno, Ceres, and other Spirits, which is thematically linked to the play's celebration of marriage, fertility, and the continuation of the royal lines of Milan and Naples.
4. The plot of Caliban, Trinculo, and Antonio is further advanced, and the two drunkards are shown for what they are, as even Caliban realizes that they are fools and that he would do better to worship other gods.
5. The scene gives occasion for Prospero's famous speech to Ferdinand and Miranda, which seems to spring out of nowhere, dramatically.

6. The plans of Prospero are carried toward a successful conclusion.

ACT V

ACT V: SCENE 1

This act, like Act IV, consists only of the relatively short Scene 1, plus the Epilogue of twenty lines of tetrameter verse, spoken by Prospero, which is believed by some commentators to be the addition of someone other than Shakespeare.

At the end of Act IV, Prospero announced that all of his enemies are now at his mercy. However, as became clear almost at the beginning of the play, Prospero always has been in control of events on the enchanted island since *The Tempest* began, so that nothing has changed from beginning to end of the play as far as his power is concerned.

In Act V, all of the characters in the play come together in the denouement (the "unknotting" of events following the major climax of the plot of a play). In *The Tempest*, since Prospero's relative power has not changed nor has he undergone any sudden reversal of fortune, good or bad, the denouement of Act V is more in the nature of a final scene in which mysteries are unraveled and misunderstandings, such as the mutual belief of Alonso and Ferdinand that the other is dead, set straight.

At six o'clock—the hour at which Prospero predicted his work would end—Prospero appears in his cell dressed in his magic garments. The King and his followers are meanwhile confined in a grove near the cell while the mariners of the King's ship are sleeping the sleep of enchantment in the ship's hold. The two drunkards and Caliban are being "driven" like wild animals in the direction of Prospero's cell, and Prospero's daughter and new son-in-law, Miranda and Ferdinand, are playing at chess, oblivious to the world.

As Ariel describes the King, he and the two guilty lords, Antonio and Sebastian, are "distracted" and unable to move, with Gonzalo, Adrian, and Francisco watching over them. If Prospero could only see them, says his servant, his affections, or disposition toward his enemies, "would become tender." Ariel says that he would be tender toward them were he human.

Prospero's answer to the observations of Ariel is quite important for the meaning of the play and might easily be overlooked in a quick reading:

Hast thou, which art but air, a touch, a feeling Of their afflictions, and shall not myself, One of their kind, that relish all as sharply Passion as they, be kindlier moved than thou art? Though with their high wrongs I am struck to th' quick, Yet with my nobler reason 'gainst my fury Do I take part. The rarer action is In virtue than in vengeance. They being penitent, The sole drift of my purpose doth extend Not a frown further. Go, release them, Ariel (lines 21–30).

Prospero's enemies have repented, and therefore the Duke will not seek revenge. His reason—the faculty in humans which they shared with the angels and with the divine principle, in the belief of most of Shakespeare's contemporaries—bids Prospero practice forgiveness rather than take revenge on his enemies.

His enemies are completely helpless in his power. But Prospero masters himself. By an effort of will, based on long study and teaching, he resists the human tendency to take revenge. There is an apparent change in Prospero's outlook in this speech at the beginning of Act V: He turns from revenge to forgiveness. But actually he has been bent on this course from the very beginning of the play. For he seems to have foreseen everything even before putting his plan into operation. His change of heart is as much an illusion as anything else on the enchanted island, and is employed as a dramatic device by Shakespeare to heighten suspense. The audience of *The Tempest* is left wondering, until Act V, as to the extent of the revenge Prospero will take on his enemies. After all, those enemies are formidable, especially Antonio.

COMMENT

The ideas in Prospero's speech are those of resignation, reconciliation, and Christian forgiveness of one's enemies. All were Elizabethan commonplaces, based on traditional religious teaching within the Judaeo-Christian ethic. The speech succeeds brilliantly not through the originality of its ideas, but rather because of the noble tone and the sheer beauty of its lines.

As Ariel exits, Prospero utters the other great soliloquy of the play spoken by him—a speech almost equal in genius to the speech on the transitoriness of the "cloud-capped towers" in Act IV. In this soliloquy, Prospero begins by addressing:

> Ye elves of hills, brooks, standing lakes, and groves, And ye that on the sands with printless foot Do chase the ebbing Neptune . . . (lines 33–34).

He continues:

> But this rough magic I here abjure; and when I have required Some heavenly music which even now I do To work mine end upon their senses that This airy charm is for, I'll break my staff, Bury it certain fathoms in the earth, And deeper than did ever plummet sound I'll drown my book (lines 50–57).

Prospero ends by requring "some heavenly music" that will soothe the troubled minds of Sebastian, Antonio, and the King and will awaken them free from the burden of that guilt for which they have repented.

COMMENT

This speech is associated by many commentators and general readers with Shakespeare's own farewell to the stage. Shakespeare did not write another complete play after *The Tempest.* He retired at the height of his powers to his home in Stratford, which he had purchased after his years of creativity in London. In this interpretation, Prospero becomes identified with Shakespeare to such an extent that some have called this great soliloquy Shakespeare's farewell to his art, to the London stage, and to the "magic" he had mastered.

We cannot know whether this thought was in Shakespeare's mind. Certainly the speech seems to lack dramatic motivation. The gravity of the lines, in which Prospero is saying that he will give up his magical powers, is far in excess of what is required by the plot of the play—even as the "cloud-capped" towers speech is in excess of the requirements of the dramatic situation. All we can say is that it is risky to identify Prospero with Shakespeare in this speech of abjuration.

At this point in Act V, Prospero does what his servant Ariel had earlier done in Act III: he notifies the three guilty "men of sin" of their crimes. Alonso had "cruelly used" Prospero and his daughter; Sebastian and Antonio had been "furtherers in the act" and had behaved remorselessly; and Antonio had acted unnaturally toward his own brother, Prospero. Both are "unnatural," because both Antonio and Sebastian would have murdered the King, a peculiarly horrible act for Shakespeare's age.

Remarking that the three noblemen would not recognize him in his magical garments, Prospero calls Ariel to him once again, promising that before long he shall have his coveted freedom, and dresses himself once again in the garments of the Duke of Milan, symbolizing his imminent return to the world and departure from the enchanted island.

COMMENT

Here the basic Elizabethan distinction between Reason and Passion, or a human's rational and animal natures, is again made clear. *The Tempest* is potentially a tragedy of usurpation and revenge: the same stuff of which *Hamlet* and *Macbeth* are made. Unbridled ambition, passion, hatred, murder, revenge, and fratricide are all present potentially in *The Tempest*, but all are dispelled and rendered harmless by the action of Prospero.

Ariel's song (lines 88–94) possesses a beauty beyond the realm of intellect.

The mariners, who have been sleeping a charmed sleep under the hatches of the King's ship, are ordered to be awakened by Ariel. Prospero presents himself to the awakening King and his company as the "wronged Duke of Milan" and embraces Alonso and Gonzalo.

Alonso shows disbelief at seeing Prospero and relief that he is alive, for the guilt of his supposed death has weighed heavily on the King. Gonzalo, too, is overcome:

> Whether this be Or not be, I'll not swear (lines 123–124).

Prospero turns to Antonio and Sebastian and tells them that he could denounce the two conspirators to their King and "justify" them as traitors—i.e., prove that they had intended to murder Alonso. But as treason would be punished by immediate execution, Prospero promises that for the moment he will tell no tales. "The devil speaks in him," observes Sebastian in an aside to Antonio. Prospero's answer is not without significance beyond its shortness, for he simply says: "No. It is not the devil, but the principle of divinity which speaks through Prospero."

> **COMMENT**
> Whereas in *Macbeth* we find a devilish magic, or black magic, sometimes called goety, in *The Tempest* we find nothing employed by Prospero except white magic, or theurgy.

Prospero demands his dukedom from his brother. It is significant that Antonio does not even answer, he is so filled with shame and guilt. He is the deepest-dyed villain in *The Tempest*, and we are left with some doubt concerning the completeness of his reformation.

After Prospero's stern reproach directed at his brother, the suspense is further built up by Shakespeare to a sort of minor climax when Ferdinand and Miranda are "discovered" playing chess.

This is, in the eyes of the beholders, "a most high miracle." The King is moved from despair to joy as he sees his son alive. Miranda exclaims:

> O, wonder! How many goodly creatures are there here! How beauteous mankind is! O brave new world That has such people in't (lines 182–185).

To which Prospero replies simply:

> 'Tis new to thee (line 186).

This has an implication that in Prospero's view his daughter will inevitably be disillusioned by the world, which is not characterized by the wise and humane control found on the enchanted island.

Gonzalo rejoices; "Was Milan thrust from Milan that his issue/ Should become kings of Naples? O, rejoice . . ." (lines 206–207). This might seem superfluous; Prospero, having demonstrated great power over Nature herself, seems a bit silly settling for a mere dukedom again. But this signifies his rejoining of human society, strengthened by his sojourn on the enchanted island and by his studies. And his descendants will be kings, not princes. Thus at the end of the play there occurs the Elizabethan equivalent of "upward mobility," as Prospero marries off his daughter to a King's son.

COMMENT

Shakespearean comedy and dramatic romance end with a marriage or the prospect of marriage. The ending of *The Tempest* follows this pattern, though it may seem relatively unsatisfactory in view of the effortless power displayed by Prospero, and the grave and stately tone of the poetry as the ruler of the island gives up his power forever to return to the world. But in a deeper sense the ending is a fit one, heralding the end of one cycle of existence, represented by Prospero and Alonso, and the beginning of a new one as Ferdinand and Miranda succeed to royal power.

The scene at the close of the play is triumphant because of the union of Ferdinand and Miranda and the strengthening of the royal houses of Naples and Milan.

The ship, which "but three glasses since" appeared to be splitting—that is, three hourglasses previously—is bravely rigged and ready to go to sea again. Alonso observes that what he has witnessed must be supernatural, and Prospero promises to make clear to the parties the "strangeness of this business." One practical consideration here might be simply that Prospero must demonstrate his use of white magic in his proceedings, rather than of black magic.

Prospero orders Ariel to set Caliban and his companions free, and they appear in their stolen clothing. Prospero reproaches Stephano for thinking that he could become King of the island. He orders Caliban to go to his, Prospero's, cell with his accomplices, and to "trim it handsomely." Caliban says that he will be wise hereafter:

> What a thrice-double ass Was I to take this drunkard for a god And worship this dull fool! (lines 295–297).

Caliban has advanced one step towards humanity. As Act V ends, Prospero promises calm seas and favorable winds, so that the ship will not only reach Naples but even catch up to the rest of the fleet, which proceeded on, believing the King's ship lost. He charges Ariel to attend to this:

> Then to the elements Be free, and fare thou well! (lines 317–318).

As the play ends, the party enters Prospero's cell, there to hear the story of his life.

SUMMARY AND CONCLUSION

Act V accomplishes the following:

1. It ties together the threads of the story, to resolve those situations that Prospero has simultaneously been organizing and controlling on the enchanted island, and to end the play in an artistically satisfying manner.
2. The play ends on a hopeful, though somewhat anticlimactic, note in this scene, with the prospective union of the royal houses of Milan and Naples likely to strengthen both realms. The scene thus accomplishes the transition back to

the world, with its cares, strivings for power, and inevitable disillusionments. Just as the first scenes of the play lead the audience to believe in the conditions of the enchanted island, so the last scene dispels these illusions and points up the dreamlike quality of the play.

3. The last act assembles all of the characters on the stage and ends with an atmosphere of reconciliation, pardon for offenses, hope for the future through the younger generation, and affirmation of the essential wonder and beauty of the "brave new world."

The Epilogue of twenty lines spoken by Prospero is considered inferior to the rest of the play. The lines are thought to have been written by someone other than Shakespeare. They duplicate, at a lower level of poetic excellence, the lines beginning with line 33 in Act V, in which Prospero renounces his magical powers.

CHARACTER ANALYSES

PROSPERO

Prospero is the play. His presence is felt continuously, even in those scenes in which he does not appear. He is the manipulator of the action and occupies the center of the stage.

In Latin, the name Prospero would mean, "I hope for." A member of English Renaissance society would generally have hoped for salvation, in the terms of Christian theology. Another meaning of his name would be "prosperity," implying that everything that he attempts will prosper.

Prospero is purified intellect. He is a "white" magician; he practices theurgy, not goety. Prospero's magic is always turned to good ends. At the end of the play Prospero seems to abdicate his role as the embodiment of pure intellect as he returns to Milan to resume his role as Duke.

The question arises: Is Prospero a renegade to the status he has throughout the play—the status of pure intellect? For an answer, we must turn to the concept advanced earlier—that everyone on the enchanted island, including even the human monster, Caliban, learns and is educated by the experience of *The Tempest* and its aftermath. That the island is a place of education and learning—not necessarily formal book learning, but learning to see more deeply into reality—is an axiom in the interpretation of this play. It might be better to describe the process the characters all go through as initiation, not simply education.

Prospero also learns. While he is master all through the play, he has learned well before its opening that a Prince cannot abdicate his responsibilities. Prospero lost his Dukedom in Milan in part because he neglected his everyday duties in favor of abstract and theoretical studies. Prospero was wrong to do so and in a way was punished by exile. But during his exile he has mastered both his own nature and his surroundings and learned what his duty is as a ruler. He is doing only what he should when he resumes his position as the ruler of Milan. In other Shakespearean plays, any ruler who abdicates or surrenders power, such as *King Lear* or *Richard II*—especially if he surrenders power voluntarily as did Lear—always comes to grief, and his act may lead not only to his own destruction but also to the ruin of the political order of the state, as nearly happens in *King Lear*. The theory of kingship held by many Elizabethans implied that once God had appointed his vice-regent in the person of a ruler, it was not for the ruler to attempt to modify God's judgments. So Prospero learns, and guided by his new and hard won knowledge, returns to the world of Milan, where "every third thought" shall be his grave. This last probably means that he will think of eternity, of his salvation, even while fulfilling his role as Duke, for he has learned on the island that the exercise of power for its own sake is nothing.

Is Prospero a tyrant? He has been described as such by a number of critics, but in the terms of the moral philosophy embodied in *The Tempest*, he is not. He suits his attitude, his response, and even his tone of voice to the person or being with whom he is dealing, whether it is Ferdinand, Ariel, Caliban, or his own daughter. This is not tyranny; it is the prudence and the control of people and situations that a wise Renaissance ruler would have been expected to demonstrate, and Prospero is every inch a ruler.

Prospero may be an allegorical figure, but only to a certain extent; we can never fully delimit his allegorical meaning. He triumphs through his practice of white magic, and in effect Shakespeare shows us the triumph of good over evil, of goodness so absolute and so well informed that it can render even the blackest plots of a villain like Antonio harmless.

Prospero embodies not only the triumph of good over evil but also the triumph of the intellect over the lower faculties. His long stay on the island has not resulted in his becoming embittered. He has managed to achieve power over the elements by the study and mastery of magic books. Prospero can be compared to a great scientist or physician of today.

It may be that Shakespeare, in having Prospero admit that he is absentminded in forgetting the plot of Caliban and his companions against his life, is emphasizing the human quality of the Duke. If he were entirely a supernatural and intellectual creature, he could not forget—but the "forgetting" is, after all, a dramatic device.

Prospero is entirely good. Despite his apparent harshness toward Caliban, he gives even the human monster a second chance to learn, to become more human, as he allows Caliban to see his two drunken companions for what they are during the progress of the plot against Prospero's life. He punishes Ferdinand solely to test him.

Although Prospero drowns his book and forswears magic at the end of the play, he has changed little except to have become a better ruler than he was when, in "the dark backward and abysm of time," he so lost touch with his realm that he was cast away by his usurping brother. While the play has little spectacular action, Prospero keeps that action under effortless control throughout.

As a final point about the character of Prospero, observe that Shakespeare has performed the difficult feat of making supreme goodness more interesting than supreme evil.

MIRANDA

Prospero's daughter, an unspoiled princess. Having no experience of the world, she does not know how to pretend or to dissemble, especially with regard to her emotions. She seems to have a minimum of contact with the supernatural forces employed by Prospero, as she evidently never sees Ariel in his own shape, whatever that is. Miranda, though she is Prospero's daughter, does not share his power over the elements and the supernatural.

Her artlessness in showing her love for Ferdinand is especially charming, while her name, as we have observed, means "worthy of admiration," which she certainly is by reason of her beauty, innocence, and consideration for Ferdinand and the other rare creatures who inhabit the brave new world she has found.

GONZALO

In some ways the most interesting of the nonsupernatural characters in the play. He corresponds to the nobleman Kent in *King Lear*, in his devotion to his king, Alonso. Though old, he is still alert, as witnessed in his observation right after the shipwreck that the clothes of his companions are still dry and whole. While the other characters may bait him and think of him as a garrulous old fool, he is far from that. Even his Ideal Commonwealth speech, tangential though it may seem to the situation at hand, is intended to cheer up his King and distract him from his grief over the supposed death of his son and heir. Gonzalo is the type of good courtier or adviser to rulers, who places his master's good above any personal advantage and even tries to protect his master from himself, as Gonzalo does during the scene in which Alonso's guilt has made him temporarily deranged.

ALONSO

The King of Naples is initially such a guilt-ridden man, stricken by such grief for the supposed loss of his son, Ferdinand, in the shipwreck, that he scarcely wishes to continue living. He is not presented as an especially forceful ruler, as otherwise he might contrast favorably with Prospero.

Alonso had been guilty of conniving with Antonio in depriving Prospero of the dukedom of Milan. This is the basic offense for which he is punished by the loss of his son. But Alonso feels genuine remorse and wishes to expiate his guilt. At the end of the play he is genuinely glad to see Prospero so that he can make amends. He is the most thoroughly reformed character in the play. We are not sure about Antonio's reformation, but we have little doubt about Alonso's.

FERDINAND

Alonso's son and heir, the Prince of Naples, and a paragon of a young prince. He upholds a romantic ideal of chivalry and honor, behaving like a prince even while, for the sake of his lady love, Miranda, he performs menial tasks. A student as well as a man of action, he becomes fascinated with his prospective father-in-law's magic. He is properly respectful toward Prospero as well as toward his own father, and simply by what he is inspires such confidence that we imagine the realms of Naples and Milan will fall into good hands when he succeeds to the throne.

SEBASTIAN

He has seen the throne of Naples go to his elder brother, Alonso. Sebastian impresses us as rather weak and easily led; he falls under the domination of the crafty Antonio. He is capable of treason, regicide, and fratricide as he enters into the plot proposed by Antonio to murder the King, Alonso, in which case Sebastian would succeed to the throne. He seems more reformed at the end of the play than Antonio does.

ANTONIO

The false Duke of Milan, who viciously usurped the place of his brother, Prospero, and set him adrift in a leaky boat with his infant daughter, hoping that they would drown. He is so "unnatural" that he would murder his own brother, without remorse, in order to gain power. He is an evil counselor, and thus is contrasted with Gonzalo, whom he mocks for an old fool. He talks the much weaker Sebastian into a plot designed to take the King's life. At the end of *The Tempest*, Antonio says nothing when Prospero requires his Dukedom back, and we are not sure how far his reformation extends.

ARIEL

An incorporeal Spirit, whose true shape is never revealed but who has the ability to be everywhere and to assume various forms, such as that of a bird or a harpy. Ariel moves easily through the four elements recognized by the Elizabethans—fire, air, water, and earth. He appears as a magic fire at the beginning of the play, in the shipwreck; he moves instantly through the air and the water; he can even move under the earth. He must be restrained continually by Prospero, because what Ariel most seeks is freedom. He was originally freed by Prospero from the black magical enchantment of "the foul witch Sycorax," who imprisoned him in a pine tree. Ariel is insubstantial, purely a Spirit. He is Prospero's executive arm; he manages the other Spirits employed by Prospero and at the end of the play is set free to return to the elements.

CALIBAN

As Ariel is delicate and incorporeal, so Caliban is gross and close to the earth. He is a fantastic human monster of indeterminate shape, variously described as a moon-calf, a tortoise, and a wild man. He has brutish desires, seeking to violate the honor of Prospero's daughter even though Prospero taught him language and in other ways has been his teacher. Caliban has a grievance, as he fancies that the island is actually his by right of succession and inheritance from his mother, the witch Sycorax. Yet paradoxically Caliban is a poet; his speeches describing the enchanted island are at times hauntingly beautiful. He worships a cruel god, Setebos.

Caliban develops during the play, to the point where he recognizes the excellence of his master when he contrasts it with the foolish drunkenness of Stephano and Trinculo. He resolves to seek grace and be wise; at the end of the play, he sees Stephano and Trinculo for what they are, and therefore he has learned.

Caliban's character is actually a complex blend of the demonological lore of Shakespeare's time and the pure poetic imagination. He is extremely superstitious and full of fear at what his master will do. Yet his character is by no means without appeal, and he is far from simply being an embodiment of evil.

TRINCULO

A Fool or Jester in the Court of Alonso, the King of Naples. Displays a low form of cunning and is always ready to turn a situation to his own advantage. He is undone by his greed when he and Stephano, roaring drunk, are led on by Ariel and the other Spirits into attempting to steal the glistening clothing from the line outside Prospero's cell. The character of Trinculo provides some comic relief within the serious action of the play.

STEPHANO

A drunken butler, also a servant of Alonso. Stephano is more aggressive than Trinculo, and it is he whom Caliban worships until he learns better. He is distracted, as is Trinculo, from the pursuit of his plot against Prospero by the clothes on the clothesline outside Prospero's cell; it is at this point that Caliban realizes the unworthiness of Stephano, who is so easily turned from his purpose by "trash."

ADRIAN AND FRANCISCO

Both are noblemen who, with Gonzalo, are attendants of Alonso. They are neutral characters, hardly distinguished one from another and with very little to say. Neither is implicated in the plot against Alonso by Sebastian and Antonio. They accompany Gonzalo as he cares for the distracted King after the charm has been placed on him by Prospero's magic.

MINOR CHARACTERS

Iris, Ceres, and Juno are supernatural beings who appear in the masque in Act IV for the delight of Ferdinand and Miranda. They have no particular character other than the mythological, but they have more than a comic purpose, for the masque is enacted in praise of marriage and fertility, and in some way all three fertility deities.

The Nymphs and Reapers are also mythological beings called up by Prospero's art to join in the masque in Act IV.

The Master of the Ship, the Boatswain, and the Sailors are seen only at the beginning and the end of the play. They are rough but entirely competent in their profession of seafaring and are, of course, baffled by the magical tempest and by the enchantments that surround them. While they are all minor characters, the conversation during the tempest, when the boat is believed to be lost, is important as it sets up the problems of authority, rulership, and responsibility with which the play deals when the King's noble servants try to interfere with the mariners in their struggle to save the ship.

CRITICAL COMMENTARY

GENERAL

The nineteenth century accepted the ideas that *The Tempest* was an allegory and Shakespeare's personal farewell to the English stage. There is evidence for both, but neither can be documented. The biographical approach was intensified by Edward Dowden, who divided Shakespeare's life on the basis of his plays into four periods. Dowden assigned *The Tempest* to the final, serene period, when, having emerged from the despair and darkness of his great tragic period, he was at peace with himself and with the world and could thus produce the calm and forgiving spirit of *The Tempest.* Shakespeare could say farewell to his art with the same nobility with which Prospero said farewell to his magic. At any rate, Dowden's view is characteristic of the Romantic biographical approach to the play.

THE SUPERNATURAL

One important consideration in approaching this play is the use of magic on the part of Prospero. Belief in demons and witches was woven into Elizabethan and Jacobean society in a way very difficult for us to imagine. It was not necessary for Shakespeare's audience to believe literally in magic and in the objective existence of witches and monsters, although many of the audience undoubtedly did.

The two plays of Shakespeare that make most use of magic and witchcraft are *The Tempest* and *Macbeth*; in general it is white magic or theurgy that is at work is *The Tempest*, leading to a good end, while in *Macbeth* the thane of Glamis and Cawdor is entrapped by the arts of black magic or goety. It may be of interest that it was not until 1736 that English law was changed to make it impossible to prosecute a person in any court for "Witchcraft, Sorcery, Inchantment, or Conjuration."

ALLEGORY

There are many allegorical interpretations of *The Tempest*. In allegory there is a one-to-one relationship between a character or event in literature and some other object or meaning. As James Russell Lowell worked out the allegory of this play, Ariel was equated with fancy, Caliban with brute understanding, and Prospero with the imagination.

A more extreme criticism was that of Miss Emma Brockway Wagner, who saw *The Tempest* as an "allegory of the Christian Reformation." Each character in the play, in this view, had a part in standing for an event in the progress of Christianity throughout a total of twelve centuries, beginning in A.D. 325. Again, there is no evidence in the play for this interpretation, and it is alluded to here simply by way of cautioning the student against being carried away by the infinite suggestibility of the play.

For Professor G. Wilson Knight the play becomes a "myth of the national soul" of England, in terms of England's instincts for rulership and her political toleration (represented by Prospero), her "inventive and poetic genius" (represented by Ariel), and finally, her colonizing activities, which led to the upgrading and the salvation of primitive peoples (represented by Caliban).

LEVELS OF REALITY

Professor Tillyard emphasizes the theme of regeneration and reconciliation in *The Tempest* and is more responsible than anyone else for the idea that the play starts out as potentially a tragedy; he finds that "Antonio is . . . one of Shakespeare's major villains," fully capable of causing the same kind of tragedy caused by Iago or the daughters of King Lear. Tillyard also discusses the "planes of reality" in *The Tempest.* But Professor Spencer goes further in pointing up the operation in the play of three hierarchical levels of Nature: animal, human, and intellectual (levels identified with various sets of characters). It is he who applies the terms *sensible, rational,* and *intellectual* to the levels of being of the play. In his approach, Caliban represents the level of mere sense, or the animal level; the plotting noblemen the level of untrustworthy reason (Antonio, after all, acts on an intellectual although certainly not on a moral level); and Prospero with his chief servant Ariel represents the level of "uncontaminated intellect."

THE ABUSE OF REASON

One point not made thus far is that the more villainous and dangerous plot is developed by Antonio and Sebastian, men who evidence a high degree of the rational faculty. Antonio is rather brilliant, but he adopts the Machiavellian view that the only reality is power and physical force. As long as he can get what he wants, he will not be bothered by conscience. Sebastian is but a weaker copy of this imperfect pattern. Caliban, on the other hand, appears at the start of the play as basically animalistic; yet he learns and becomes better. He is not a human and is not expected to operate at the same level of rationality that one would expect of a nobleman such as Antonio. Therefore, it might be said that he actually rises to a point that is morally superior to Antonio and Sebastian. He is a serious as well as a humorous character.

ESSAY QUESTIONS AND ANSWERS

Question
What does the character of Prospero signify?

Answer
Prospero embodies the virtues that Shakespeare's audience expected of a ruler—magnanimity, the ability to elicit obedience and to control the behavior of his subjects based on his superior intellectual, rational, and moral powers. Prospero's magical powers represent his ability to master his environment and all other beings on his enchanted island.

Prospero, by mastering his passion for revenge on his enemies, proves a human's ability to control his or her own actions by an effort of will. Prospero represents at least the possibility of free will. Even when Prospero is a stern ruler, as in his dealings with Caliban and with his own evil brother, Antonio, he is never a tyrant; he metes out justice with mercy.

Question
How is Prospero related to his servants Ariel and Caliban?

Answer
If Prospero represents the highest intellectual faculty of a human being, Ariel may represent the spirited faculty—the executive arm of the intellect—which must always be controlled by the intellect. Similarly, Caliban may represent the animal passions, which also must be under the control of reason and the intellect.

Both Ariel and Caliban need constantly to be restrained by Prospero, and in each case, Prospero fits the kind of restraint needed to the particular character with whom he is dealing, as he generally does on the enchanted island. Thus, he threatens Caliban when the human monster is rebellious toward him; he also threatens Ariel, but in a milder way, when Ariel seeks his freedom before his time is out and before the work begun in *The Tempest* is accomplished.

Question

May it be said that *The Tempest* is potentially another great Shakespearean tragedy? If so, how does it differ from tragedy?

Answer

The answer to the first question is yes. At the beginning of the play, there is a potential tragic situation, especially as Antonio, a villain cast in the mold of an Iago, formulates his plot against the life of Alonso, King of Naples.

The plot is foiled because Prospero is already in control through his magic arts and his supernatural servants of everything and everybody on the enchanted island. No harm can come to anyone but by Prospero's permission, and after an apparent brief struggle with himself, Prospero resolves that the "rarer action is in virtue than in vengeance." Thus, he decides not to take revenge on Antonio and Sebastian, which would have led to a revenge tragedy.

The action of the play is resolved quite early. Evil is disarmed unknown to itself, whereas in the great Shakespearean tragedies, evil burns itself out in an action that destroys good as well as evil. In *The Tempest*, the good are safeguarded from harm, and the tragedy remains only potential; it cannot become actual.

Question

What is the function of the Alonso-Sebastian-Antonio plot? Likewise, what is the function of the Caliban-Trinculo-Stephano plot?

Answer

Both plots heighten suspense in what would else be a rather static situation, since Prospero is so much in control of what happens on the island. Suspense is aroused as the audience wonders whether the attempt on the life of Alonso, or that on the life of Prospero, can be successful. Of course it cannot be, but Shakespeare underplays Prospero's supreme powers at first, so that we wonder if he does have complete control.

Further, the two plots, which balance each other on the serious and the comic levels respectively, illustrate the educative action of *The Tempest.* The six characters involved learn what their moral duty is; they are changed for the better, with the possible exception of Prospero's brother, Antonio, who is the major villain of the play.

At the level of allegory, both sets of characters represent a human being's imperfect nature undergoing the discipline through the enforced initiation into the deeper realities of existence by Prospero's magic.

Question

How does Shakespeare obtain in the readers or the audience of *The Tempest* "that willing suspension of disbelief which constitutes poetic faith"?

Answer

The primary answer to this question involves the frame of the "real world" that Shakespeare establishes at the beginning of the play. We are led away from the beginning situation—which occurs in the midst of reality, a storm at sea, with mariners fighting desperately for their lives—by more or less imperceptible gradations, until we come to accept Prospero's magic as a "natural" thing. By the end of Act I, Shakespeare has completed the dramatic exposition of the conditions on the enchanted island so perfectly that we are prepared to accept any marvels as everyday occurrences.

Question
What evidence is there that the play contains allegorical elements?

Answer
The evidence primarily comes from the moral philosophy professed by most thinkers in the Elizabethan age. A human being's soul was generally thought of as multileveled, having sensible, rational, and intellectual faculties. In terms of their dramatic functions as well as their utterances in the play, Prospero, Ariel, and Caliban must in some way form an allegorical representation of the three aspects of a human being's nature, whatever the terms used to describe these levels. Many of the speeches, especially of Prospero, are not motivated dramatically, and it is hard to escape the conclusion that they have allegorical or symbolic content. The danger in interpreting *The Tempest* lies in the temptation to assign meanings too rigidly and too specifically to Prospero, Ariel, and Caliban.

Question
What is meant by the statement that *The Tempest*, alone among the plays of Shakespeare, strictly observes the dramatic unities?

Answer
The three unities found in the classical drama especially of the Greeks and in certain later periods were those of time, place, and action. In most of his plays Shakespeare did not observe them at all. The unity of time was a concept that specified that in a play all of the action should be confined as closely as possible to the circuit of a single sun. Extreme purists insisted that the play could last no longer chronologically than the exact time of the action on the stage, to main-

tain the illusion of reality. *The Tempest* apparently covers no more than four hours, and Shakespeare makes constant reference, through Prospero and Ariel, to the passage of time so that he makes the unity of time conspicuous.

As to the unity of place, everything takes place on a supposedly deserted island, except the storm in Act I, Scene I, and even that takes place so close to the island that it qualifies. The unity of place is thus exceptionally well observed in the play. The unity of action specifies that there should be no irrelevancies in the play and that all digressions and subplots should be avoided. Shakespeare has something of a subplot in the persons of Stephano, Trinculo, and possibly Caliban, but at the same time these are all tied together by the plot against the master of the enchanted island, Prospero.

It may be that in view of the fantastic plot and action of the play, Shakespeare observed the unities to increase the truthfulness of its effect and further lead the audience to suspend disbelief.

Question
What are the elements of fertility ritual or marriage celebration in the play?

Answer
Primarily these relate to the masque celebrating the betrothal of Ferdinand and Miranda in Act IV and the affirmation of the proposed marriage in Act V. This is an important thread in the play, for the marriage signals a return to the reality of the outer world; it is basically hopeful, for we have been convinced that Ferdinand and Miranda are fit rulers to succeed to the thrones of Naples and Milan. It is hoped by all among the principals of the play that the marriage will prove fruitful; this was especially important in the case of a royal house, because if there were no heirs, the line and the succession to the power would soon pass into other hands.

Question

How is suspense maintained in the play, even though Prospero is in control of everything at all times?

Answer

Shakespeare resolves this problem by keeping many of the strands of Prospero's control out of sight—they are present by implication. He uses the slightly clumsy device of having Prospero "forget" the plot of Caliban against his life, and he allows the plot of Antonio and Sebastian to come near to threatening the life of Alonso. By the time we realize the full power of Prospero, the play is near its conclusion.

Question

How is the problem of evil resolved in the play; is evil destroyed in the struggle on the island?

Answer

The problem of evil is not resolved in the play; probably it could never be, even in that enchanted realm. What happens is that evil is overcome by the actions of those who are good.

There are several different kinds of evil in this play, generally manifested by specific people. We have political evil in the characters of Alonso (to the least degree), Sebastian (who does not succeed), and Antonio, who has actually committed the ultimate political sin of usurpation, and as far as he knows has also committed murder. The next kind is the evil of the flesh, manifested by Stephano and Trinculo as drink and greed. They are readily turned aside from an even greater evil, that of murder, by the sight of rich clothes hanging on a clothes line. Caliban also manifests this kind of evil in his reported attempt to rape Miranda. But by the end of the play he will "sue for grace."

By the end of the play all these characters are punished for the evil they have committed, or have intended to commit. Alonso thinks he has lost his son, Antonio fears vengeance from his forgiving brother. But these intellectual and political crimes are punished more than those of the flesh. Caliban will be wracked with agues, and the drunken courtiers have their ardent spirits dampened by immersion in a horsepond. Their desires are thus soon quenched.

Question

May it be said that all on the enchanted island are in some way educated—given deeper insights into reality—during *The Tempest*?

Answer

Yes indeed! The Island possesses the educational value of an academy devoted to the study of morals, and in particular to the study of good and evil. At the beginning of the play the characters are set very clearly before us in terms of their respective attitudes to virtue. The moral states of the visitors to the Island, for instance, are shown to us through their individual vision of the landscape in Act II, Scene 1. Adrian, the neutral, notes the freshness of the air of the Island, while Sebastian and Antonio claim that it is full of foul smells. Similarly, Gonzalo, the man of virtue who saved Prospero and Miranda, notes "How lush and lusty the grass looks! how green!" Sebastian and Antonio, by contrast, see only parched land. In short, the Island is obviously enchanted, because all see it according to the amount of personal virtue they possess.

Gradually, in the course of the play, the nature of good and evil is shown to us, and those who have done wrong are punished for their faults. Alonso, whose evil action was to aid Antonio in his usurpation of the dukedom of Milan, is in turn plotted against by his brother, Sebastian, and also the usurper, Antonio. He awakens from his dream to the literal reality of armed men standing over him.

In the same way, Gonzalo is again reawakened to the existence of evil in the world, and by the apparent death of Ferdinand, he sees the punishment inflicted upon Alonso. The King of Naples sees this for himself, and the more Gonzalo speaks of the advantageous marriage that the King had made for his daughter, Claribel, the more the King reproaches himself for having sent his daughter far away. This match has obviously been one for money and position, and for his ambition, Alonso believes himself bereft of his son as well.

Ferdinand and Miranda also learn. They discover the nature of virtuous love. At the same time, Miranda's knowledge of evil is reinforced, and the test of Ferdinand is not merely one of his constancy in love but of his virtue as well. Both young people are shown in the process of physical and emotional maturing.

Caliban, the creature of the earth, learns too. When he says at the end of the play that he will sue for grace, he is showing that he has discovered that fine clothes are not in themselves a guarantee of a gentleman, or of virtue. He has learned to look beneath the appearance and can appreciate Prospero as his master now that he has seen the two courtiers, Stephano and Trinculo. These two characters have probably also learned. Their punishment of being led through a horsepond is one fitting their bestial natures. In effect, they are punished more than anyone else in the play; probably Shakespeare saw them as worse than the others, because they willingly permitted themselves to give in to the desires of their flesh and have become like animals.

Prospero himself learns, and he is taught by Ariel, the creature of the air. Initially it appears that Prospero planned to take vengeance on his enemies, but Ariel notes that even he would feel pity for the court party if he were human. At this implied rebuke, Prospero—whose abilities and knowledge are greater in effect than Ariel's, because he possesses a soul—swallows his wrath and forgives his enemies.

Question

Is the conclusion of the play properly motivated and intellectually satisfying?

Answer

It is if one views it against the background of Elizabethan political and philosophical thought. While it may appear to be a comedown for Prospero to resume his governing of Milan after having exercised supreme power on his island, this is still a socially superior role for him—a role in which he originally failed, as witness to the usurpation of his brother, Antonio. Prospero voluntarily assumes the burdens of office again. Life must continue in the real world. This is symbolized by the marriage of Ferdinand and Miranda and the prospect of the union and continuance of the royal lines of Naples and Milan. The play, then, has a cyclical quality; it returns to a bright reality at the end.

BIBLIOGRAPHY

Bowling, Lawrence E. "The Theme of Natural Order in *The Tempest.*" *College English*, XII (1951), 203–209.

Cawley, Robert Ralston. "Shakespeare's Use of the Voyagers." *PMLA*, XLI (1926), 688–726.

———. *The Voyagers and Elizabethan Drama.* Boston: D. C. Heath, 1938.

Chambers, E. K. "The Integrity of *The Tempest.*" *Review of English Studies*, I (1925), 129–150.

Dowden, Edward. *Shakespeare: A Critical Study of His Mind and His Art.* New York: Harper & Brothers, 1 (1873); reprinted by Barnes and Noble, Inc., 1965.

Gesner, Carol. "*The Tempest* as Pastoral Romance." *Shakespeare Quarterly*, V (1959), 531–539.

Gilbert, A. H. "*The Tempest*: Parallelism in Characters and Situations." *Journal of English and Germanic Philology*, XIV (1915), 63–74.

Hankins, John E. "Caliban the Bestial Man." *PMLA*, LXII (1947), 793–801.

Hart, J. A., Jr. "*The Tempest.*" In Carnegie Institute of Technology, Pittsburgh, Department of English. *Shakespeare: Lectures on Five Plays.* Pittsburgh, 1958.

Kermode, Frank. *William Shakespeare, the Final Plays*: Pericles, Cymbeline, The Winter's Tale, The Tempest, The Two Noble Kinsmen. London: Longmans, Green & Co. for the British Council, 1961. "Writers and Their Work, No. 155."

———, ed. *The Tempest,* in the "Arden Edition of the Works of William Shakespeare." Cambridge, MA: Harvard University Press, 1958.

Knight, G. Wilson. *The Shakespearean Tempest.* London: Humphrey Milford for the Oxford University Press, 1932.

Lee, Sidney. "Caliban's Visits to England." *Cornhill Magazine,* N.S., XXXIV (1913), 333–345.

Major, John M. "Comus and *The Tempest.*" *Shakespeare Quarterly,* X (1959), 177–183.

Marx, Leo. "Shakespeare's American Fable." *Massachusetts Review,* II (1962), 40–71.

Newell, W. W. "The Source of Shakespeare's Tempest." *Journal of American Folklore,* XVI (1913), 234–257.

Nosworthy, J. M. "The Narrative Sources of *The Tempest.*" *Review of English Studies,* XXIV (1948), 281–284.

Rose, Brian W. "*The Tempest*: A Reconsideration of Its Meaning." *English Studies in Africa,* I (1958), 205–216.

Smith, Irwin. "Ariel as Ceres." *Shakespeare Quarterly,* IX (1958), 430–432.

Spencer, Theodore. *Shakespeare and the Nature of Man.* New York: Macmillan, 1958.

Spurgeon, Caroline. *Shakespeare's Imagery and What It Tells Us.* Boston: Beacon Press, 1958.

Taylor, George C. "Shakespeare's Use of the Idea of the Beast in Man." *Studies in Philology.* XLII (1943), 530–543.

Tillyard, E. M. W. *Shakespeare's Last Plays.* London: Chatto and Windus, 1938.

———. *The Elizabethan World Picture.* New York: The Macmillan Company, 1948.

Traversi, Derek A. *Shakespeare: The Last Phase.* New York: Harcourt, Brace, 1955.

———. "*The Tempest.*" *Scrutiny,* XV (1949), 127–157.

Wagner, Emma Brockway. *Shakespeare's* The Tempest*: An Allegorical Interpretation.* Yellow Springs, Ohio: Antioch Press, 1933.

Welsford, Enid. *The Court Masque.* Cambridge, England: Cambridge University Press, 1927.

Wilson, Harold S. "Action and Symbol in *Measure for Measure* and *The Tempest.*" *Shakespeare Quarterly,* IV (1953), 375–384.

NOTES

NOTES

NOTES

NOTES